THE THIRD ARMY

Joe Sutton

BROADWAY PLAY PUBLISHING INC
224 E 62nd St, NY, NY 10065
www.broadwayplaypub.com
info@broadwayplaypub.com

THE THIRD ARMY
© Copyright 2006 by Joe Sutton

First printing: August 2006
I S B N: 0-88145-295-5

Book design: Marie Donovan
Word processing: Microsoft Word
Typographic controls: Ventura Publisher
Typeface: Palatino
Printed and bound in the U S A

CHARACTERS & SETTING

PAVEL MAREK, *Czech, thirties*
DIANE BRODSKY, *American, late thirties*
LUBOMIR "LUBO" BRODSKY, *Czech/American, fifties*
BARRY AXELROD, *American, late forties*
ALISON CRAWFORD, *American, mid twenties*

Place: Karlovec, a small town in the Czech Republic; also, early on, in Prague

Time: The first years after the Velvet Revolution

SCENES

A word about the setting: Because of the many locations, the settings in each instance should be simply suggested. Even the hunting lodge, the location to which we most often return, should be established quite simply, allowing us to move in and out of it in a matter of moments.

In addition to these rather spare scenic requirements, there may also be a slide projection system used at the beginning.

A note about the text: A dash in the text (—) indicates an interrupted speech. An ellipsis (...) indicates that the speaker trails off.

SLIDES

Slide 1: TEMELIN (Teh-mah-leen)—a Chernobyl-style nuclear plant located smack in the center of Europe, forty miles from the Austrian border.

Slide 2: Built originally by the Soviets, this plant, like so many others in Eastern Europe, was left half-finished and unattended when the wall came down.

Slide 3: With the new government in charge, there arose two central questions:

Slide 4: Would construction resume?

Slide 5: Which Western firm would get the job that might, in the end, when all other plants were taken into account, amount to billions of dollars worth of contracts?

to Tomas

GLOSSARY—GUIDE TO PRONUNCIATION

Pavel Marek (Pah'-vul Mah'-rek)

Lubo Brodsky (Loo'-boh Brahd'-ski)

Temelin (Teh'-mah-leen) a nuclear plant in Southern Bohemia

Becherovska (Beck'-er-of-kah) a ginger flavored brandy

Na zdravi (Nah zdrah'-vee) "to your health"

Karlovec (Karl'-oh-vets) a fictional town in South Bohemia

U Kralu (Ooo Krah'-loo) a beer hall in Prague

Dukovany (Duke'-oh-vah-nee) a small town in Moravia with a nuclear waste dump

Krauthamer (Kraut'-ham-mer)

Sarka Rebanova (Shark'-ah Ray'-bahn-oh-vah)

Vacha (Vah'-kah)

Jiri (Year'-zhee)

Hasek (Hahsh'-eck)

Holub (Hol'-ub)

Franticiek Dudek (Frahn'-ti-czeck Doo'-dek)

ACT ONE

Scene One

(On a balcony outside the house of culture, PAVEL MAREK *leans against a stone balustrade smoking a cigarette. He is also tapping his fingers, idly keeping time to the polka music wafting out from the ballroom inside.)*

(Distractedly flicking his cigarette into the bushes below, he immediately lights up another, beginning to pace as soon as he does. Clearly something is on his mind. But before he can consider it further, he is startled from his reverie by the sudden rather loud appearance of DIANE BRODSKY, *who comes tripping onto the balcony having just lost her heel.)*

DIANE: Oh, for Christ's sake! *(Carrying a handbag and dressed in an evening gown, this is a woman who in other circumstances might appear rather elegant. In these circumstances, she appears rather drunk. And that detracts.)* Can you believe it? *(She laughs.)* Where'd that thing go? *(She looks around. Then back at him.)* You see it?

MAREK: Pardon?

DIANE: My heel. I lost my heel.

MAREK: Ah, I see. No, I am sorry. I didn't.

(Straightening up, DIANE *looks over at him, noticing when she does his surprisingly attractive, if somewhat outdated ensemble of sports coat and slacks. It goes with his accent, which is pronounced.)*

DIANE: *(Feigning impatience)* Well, would you mind helping me?

(Half-bowing, MAREK begins to look. DIANE on the other hand, doesn't. She instead looks at him.)

DIANE: It just happened. It has to be...somewhere near here.

MAREK: *(Triumphant)* Ah! Here it is!

(Turning back and expecting to see her coming forward, he instead finds her staring at him, the frankness of her appraisal causing him to laugh a bit self-consciously. After a moment, she smiles.)

DIANE: Thanks.

MAREK: You are welcome.

(At this, she holds out her hand, and after hesitating a moment, MAREK crosses. Offering her the heel, she instead takes hold of his hand. And again she smiles.)

DIANE: Listen, would you...help me over to the railing?

(Gesturing to the balustrade, she puts her arm around his shoulder, hopping along as he guides her over.)

DIANE: Thanks again.

MAREK: Again, you are welcome.

(Slight pause)

DIANE: So. How's it going?

MAREK: *(Eager)* Fine. Very good.

DIANE: Everything you thought it would be?

MAREK: *(Confused)* I...

DIANE: *(Gesturing with her head)* Inside.

MAREK: *(Quick)* Oh. Yes.

(Again, he laughs, not sure how to take her.)

DIANE: Loud though, huh? *(Waiting)* Loud?

MAREK: Well, I... *(Again, the laugh)*

DIANE: Not that I don't like it. I do. It's just I feel like I'm going to have a brain embolism. *(Waiting for the laugh—she continues)* Listen, would you do me a favor and close those?

MAREK: Close...?

DIANE: The doors. And then come right back. I want to talk to you.

(Crossing to the double doors, MAREK pulls them closed. And for the first time since the start of the scene it is quiet.)

DIANE: Oh, Christ, that's a relief. Thank you. Thank you.

(Again MAREK bows slightly as he returns.)

DIANE: Say, listen, would you like a drink?

MAREK: *(Begging off)* I...

DIANE: Oh, come on, have a drink. *(She opens her purse, rummaging through it.)*

DIANE: Let's see, where...ah, here we are. *(She pulls out a flask.)* Good old American Jack. You like Jack?

MAREK: I...

DIANE: Jack Daniels. American whiskey. Jack.

MAREK: Oh, yes. I like it.

DIANE: Of course, you like it. What's not to like? *(She starts to pour)* Of course, I like yours, too. What do you call it? Becherovka?

MAREK: Becherovka, yes. It is good.

DIANE: *(Handing him the tumbler)* There you go.

(MAREK holds the drink, embarrassed.)

MAREK: *(Finally)* Na zdravi. *(He throws back the drink.)*

DIANE: *(Overlap)* What's that?

MAREK: Na zdravi. To your health.

DIANE: Oh. *(Having poured herself a drink, she now holds it up)* Na zdravi. *(And she too kicks it back, taking a big, contented breath after she does. And again, she smiles.)*

DIANE: Listen, you want a smoke? Cigarette?

(Already rummaging in her purse, she holds out the pack and he shakes his head. DIANE laughs.)

DIANE: American cigarettes, American whiskey. *(She lights up.)* I must be American, huh?

MAREK: *(Trying hard)* Your...we are...very happy you Americans are here.

DIANE: *(Beat, amused)* Well, we're happy to be here.

(He half bows, embarrassed.)

DIANE: *(Drunk)* So tell me, what do you stand for?

MAREK: Pardon?

DIANE: *(Waving)* This group. This...party.

MAREK: Oh. I... *(Again, he laughs, uneasily.)*

DIANE: You don't know?

MAREK: It is difficult to say.

DIANE: Well, isn't that a problem?

MAREK: I don't understand.

DIANE: Well, how do you get people to join you? If you don't know what you stand for?

MAREK: Perhaps we are not interested.

DIANE: Come again.

MAREK: In having people join us.

DIANE: Well, now I'm really lost. You don't want people to join you?

MAREK: You see, as I say, this is very complicated.

DIANE: Well, how complicated can it be? You're a political party, you're...right, you're made out of people!

MAREK: Actually—

DIANE: Here, let's have another. *(She starts to pour.)*

MAREK: I—

DIANE: Ah, come on. Here.

(She hands him the tumbler, and after a sigh, he drinks it down.)

DIANE: No, really, explain it to me. I don't understand.

MAREK: You see—

DIANE: I mean, one way or another, you gotta stand for something. Right? It may be difficult to explain, but you gotta stand for *something*. Or put it this way, why not join another group? Why join yours and not another? *(She gives him a shrug before pouring out another drink and immediately slugging it down.)*

MAREK: *(Finally)* I think the people are—

DIANE: You like the people?

MAREK: Pardon?

DIANE: The people. You like them?

MAREK: Yes.

DIANE: Well, there you are then. Then you're a people's party.

MAREK: No. For us, that is very...different.

DIANE: It's too much like the Communists.

MAREK: Yes.

DIANE: So then, what? You like the people...but you're not a people's party. You're... *(Again, she holds out her hands as if to say, "what?")*

MAREK: Actually, I—

DIANE: Look, you gotta help me with this, O K? I gotta understand this.

MAREK: *(Quick)* Why?

DIANE: What?

MAREK: *(Sharp)* Why? Why do you have to understand?

(DIANE freezes for a moment, for the first time aware that he is angry.)

DIANE: *(Off-guard)* I don't know. Because I'm here. *(Slight pause)*

MAREK: There are some things—

DIANE: Look, is this personal with you? Your political party? Are you...I mean, am I treading on...is this personal?

MAREK: No. *(Slight pause)* No, it is just difficult. To explain.

(Slight pause)

MAREK: But I will try. We do not want—

DIANE: Here, can you—

MAREK: *(Loud, sharp)* Will you let me explain? Please? You asked me to explain. Let me explain. *(He takes a moment, gathering his thoughts)* At this point right now our party is new. We are...it is important that we remain open. To ideas...to...that we have not closed our minds. *(The ideas are tumbling out, uncertainly, without confidence)* We are borrowing. Some from here, some from there. And so the answer to your question, "What do we stand for?" it is difficult. It is...not one

thing. It...there are many things. New things.
Combinations. They—

DIANE: Could—

MAREK: What?

DIANE: I'm sorry. Could... *(Shy)* ...I'd just like to get up
here. Could you help me?

MAREK: *(Confused)* Help...?

DIANE: Just...

(She gestures to her side and he comes close.)

DIANE: ...that's it, put your hand there...

(He does.)

DIANE: ...and...up!

*(He lifts her as she jumps and once on the balustrade she
finds herself close to him. She smiles, releasing him.)*

DIANE: I'm sorry. You were saying.

MAREK: *(Distracted, unsure)* I...

DIANE: You see in America you got two parties.
The Republicans and the Democrats.

MAREK: I know.

DIANE: *(Overlapping)* And everyone knows what they
STAND for. You know? It doesn't matter where you go,
what part of the country you're in, Democrats are for
government, Republicans are not.

MAREK: I know.

DIANE: But here it's like a fucking mystery. I mean,
I've had this conversation before. And every one of
you says the same thing. "It's complicated." And I'm
sure it is. But I mean, you know...at some point you
gotta be able to explain it.

MAREK: *(Cold)* At some point, I am sure we will.

(Slight pause)

DIANE: Oh, boy. Now you're angry at me, huh? Look, I'll tell you something. You want to know the truth? Come here. Come over here, I'm not going to bite you. Come here!

(This last she says sharply, drunkenly, causing him to come, reluctantly.)

DIANE: You know why I'm talking to you about this? I don't give a fuck about your politics. You want to keep 'em a secret, go ahead. You know why I'm talking to you? *(Leaning in close, widening her eyes)* Cause I want to fuck you. I want to lean over and pull you into me, and stick my tongue down your throat. What do you say?

(He shakes his head, declining.)

MAREK: I...

DIANE: Come on, you're not married, are you? Are you married?

MAREK: No.

DIANE: So then, what's the problem? What's—

MAREK: You...are married.

DIANE: But that's not a problem.

MAREK: I am sorry, I—

DIANE: *(Irked)* O K, wait a minute. Let me understand this. My being married is a problem for you?

MAREK: Yes.

DIANE: I see. But otherwise, you'd fuck me?

MAREK: Yes. I...think perhaps, yes.

DIANE: Oh, you think perhaps yes, huh?

MAREK: Yes.

(She laughs, then pulls him in close.)

DIANE: How 'bout a little kiss then? *(Breathy)* Just for friendship?

(Standing very close to her now, MAREK finds himself becoming aroused.)

MAREK: I...

DIANE: *(Murmuring)* Come on. No tongues. Just...lips.

(Their kiss, which does start out soft, quickly becomes far more serious. Until finally, again, MAREK breaks away.)

MAREK: Please, I—

DIANE: *(Breathless)* Let's go somewhere.

MAREK: No.

DIANE: Just down there. Next to the wall.

MAREK: I can't!

(About to pull MAREK into her, DIANE suddenly shouts, alarmed by the sight of a man in the doorway.)

DIANE: My God, Lubo, what the hell are you doing?

LUBO: Same thing as always, sweetheart. Looking for you.

(Speaking with a noticeable accent, LUBO BRODSKY suddenly bounds onto the balcony towards MAREK.)

LUBO: And I find you with an admirer.

MAREK: I am sorry. I—

LUBO: I am Lubo Brodsky. Diana's husband.

DIANE: And this is—

LUBO: Please, Diana. Let the young man talk for himself.

MAREK: Pavel Marek.

LUBO: *(Hard)* Pavel Marek?

MAREK: Yes.

DIANE: Pavel and I—

LUBO: *(Aggressive)* You know, Pavel, there was a time when I would have been very jealous by this. To find you alone with my wife on a balcony. Now I do not. Do you know why?

(MAREK shakes his head.)

LUBO: Because I have other fish to fry. *(Beat, smiling)* Do you know what that means?

(Again, MAREK shakes his head.)

LUBO: Where there is one... *(He looks at DIANE)* ...there is always another. *(He looks back at the hall.)*

DIANE: Oh, Lubo, how gallant.

(LUBO leans close, chuckling.)

LUBO: So you see, you are lucky.

(Slight pause)

MAREK: I—

LUBO: But tell me, Pavel, seriously, what brings you to the balcony, to be alone with my wife?

MAREK: I—

DIANE: Politics.

LUBO: *(Turning, surprised)* What's that?

DIANE: We were discussing politics.

LUBO: *(Laughing)* Oh now, that is too funny. That is too, too funny. Is that true, Pavel? Were you talking politics with my wife?

MAREK: *(Small)* Yes.

LUBO: And what did she say?

DIANE: He said to me. About his party. *(To MAREK)* Tell him.

MAREK: I—

LUBO: Wait a minute. Pavel Marek?

MAREK: Yes.

LUBO: Of Karlovec?

MAREK: Yes.

LUBO: You are Mayor of Karlovec?

MAREK: Yes.

(At this, LUBO guffaws.)

MAREK: I don't understand.

LUBO: You did not hear me before. Did you? When I told you my name. I am Lubo Brodsky. Of C D I. We are meeting tomorrow.

(And as soon as he hears this, MAREK blanches, understanding in a flash what a mistake he has made.)

MAREK: Oh, my—

LUBO: *(Laughing)* Now, tell me, is this not funny?

MAREK: I—

LUBO: Is this not incredibly funny?

DIANE: Hilarious.

LUBO: I mean, to think of it, darling. In all this country, with all its people, that he should pick you.

DIANE: I picked him.

LUBO: Of course, you did, darling. I know. But still... *(He turns to MAREK.)* ...the coincidence is startling.

(Slight pause)

MAREK: I am sorry.

LUBO: No need. No need to apologize. I would do the same.

(An awkward silence)

DIANE: So—

LUBO: So Pavel Marek, the Mayor of Karlovec, on the balcony with my wife. I should be honored.

DIANE: Lubo, for God's sake, drop it, will you?

(Ignoring DIANE, LUBO *steps closer.)*

LUBO: You know what I am thinking? Since we know each other now. Since we are friends. Why not come to my *home* tomorrow? Instead of the office.

MAREK: I—

LUBO: Please. Don't say no. *(Beat)* We would have such fun.

(Pause)

MAREK: *(Finally)* All right.

*(*LUBO *smiles at this, then suddenly slaps down his hand on the railing.)*

LUBO: I am telling you something. I am telling you something right now! *(A dramatic pause)* We...three... *(Drawing a circle around the three)* ...are going to be great friends. I feel it in my heart. Like I did with Diana the first time we met. *(Beat)* Do you believe me?

MAREK: *(Forced)* Yes, maybe.

(Again, LUBO *chuckles.)*

LUBO: No, you don't. I see you don't. But it's true. *(Pause)* However, Rome was not built in a day, and neither can we build our friendship. Diana, we must go!

DIANE: I—

LUBO: No, no. No argument. We have kept Mister Marek long enough. *(To* MAREK*)* Haven't we?

MAREK: I—

LUBO: You have others to see here tonight, I imagine. In your party. Your political party.

MAREK: *(Beat)* Yes.

LUBO: So. *(Smiles)* We'll let you do it. Diana?

DIANE: I'll...get my purse. *(She limps towards the railing.)*

LUBO: Oh now, this is interesting. *(Laughing)* What's this, darling? A war wound?

DIANE: I broke my heel... *(Adding sarcastically)* ...thanks for asking. *(She stops, taking off her shoes.) And Mister Marek was kind enough to help me find it.*

LUBO: Was he?

(He turns to MAREK as DIANE returns with her purse.)

LUBO: It's just as I thought then, isn't it?

(He holds out his hand to MAREK.)

LUBO: Great friends.

(They shake.)

LUBO: I'll call you tomorrow. With directions.

(And now DIANE holds out her hand.)

DIANE: Mister Marek.

(MAREK bows as he shakes.)

MAREK: Madam.

(LUBO watches the two of them, then smiles at MAREK.)

LUBO: Tomorrow.

(And with that, LUBO quickly escorts DIANE away— with MAREK looking after them. A moment then passes once they're gone—and MAREK turns back to the railing, the full impact of what's about to occur just then sinking in.)

(Blackout. End Scene One)

Scene Two

(An office in Prague. BARRY AXELROD *sweeps in after* ALISON CRAWFORD. *Their conversation, which had begun in the hallway, continues without pause. It is bright and energetic and clearly both are enjoying it.)*

BARRY: I'm flattered you asked.

ALISON: You can't be surprised.

BARRY: Actually, I am. First of all, I'm usually the one doing the interviewing.

*(*ALISON *is about to sit down.)*

BARRY: No, over here. *(He pulls out a second chair, this one nearer his desk. Then, continuing)* And secondly, I'm... *(Laughing, self-conscious)* ...I don't consider myself newsworthy.

ALISON: Well then, you don't know how you're perceived.

BARRY: How do you mean?

ALISON: You're a hero.

BARRY: Oh, please.

ALISON: I'm serious. To us, at least.

BARRY: In what way?

ALISON: Well, you were here first. You were doing what we're doing twenty years ago. Actually, that understates it. You were doing what we're *trying* to do twenty years ago; and you were doing it better. And now you're head of, what, the largest English language newspaper in Eastern Europe. You have a radio station. You're starting a...I hear you're starting a satellite network.

BARRY: *(Smiling, amused)* We're talking.

ALISON: I mean, my God!

(Holding out her hands, ALISON seems clearly in awe of him. BARRY smiles, his rumpled suit in marked contrast to ALISON's "uniform"—which is standard issue Gen X [i.e. ripped jeans, torn t-shirt, string bracelet.])

ALISON: *(Then, earnestly)* And all from a position of incredible integrity.

BARRY: *(Ducking his head)* Well. *(Then, immediately)* Listen, what can I get you? Can I get you a drink?

ALISON: Sure.

BARRY: Anything in particular?

ALISON: Whatever you're having.

(BARRY heads for a liquor cabinet. ALISON looks over his office.)

ALISON: *(Then, after a beat)* Is that...? Who is that over there? *(She points.)*

BARRY: Which?

ALISON: On the wall. By the cabinet.

BARRY: *(Acknowledging, glancing over)* That's Havel.

ALISON: You know Havel?

BARRY: Quite well. *(Turning back, with a smile)* Once. Quite well. *(He heads back with a drink.)*

BARRY: Actually, that picture is twenty-four years old now. At the time we were...well, I won't say we were close, but...we were working together.

ALISON: On the journal?

BARRY: On the journal, on...stuff, on—

ALISON: Well, that's actually what I want to talk to you about. *(She points to her bag.)*

ALISON: Do you mind if I...?

(BARRY *shakes his head, he doesn't mind.* ALISON *pulls out a tape recorder.*)

ALISON: I mean, it's all...I guess it's all bunched together really. The politics, the culture. Actually, maybe that's a good place to start. How do you consider yourself? Are you...would you call yourself a political person, a cultural person? Are—?

BARRY: I'm a journalist. Really. At heart.

ALISON: Well, certainly you're more than that.

BARRY: How do you mean?

ALISON: Well, I mean, besides your newspaper, you have...other interests as well.

BARRY: Such as?

ALISON: Such as politics for one. You've always been interested in politics.

BARRY: My newspaper—

ALISON: Before your newspaper. With your journal, you were...weren't you involved?

BARRY: I was then, yes. Today...I'm a journalist.

ALISON: Well, can we talk about then? I mean, I'm interested...I can't tell you how interested I am in what you're doing now... (*Taking a moment*) ...but I'm also interested in then. (*Playful, tentative*) Can we start there?

(BARRY *shrugs.*)

BARRY: Sure.

ALISON: You got here in...? (*She has taken out a pad.*)

BARRY: '68. (*Then*) Early '68. I was just out of school, like you, and...well, I won't go into details, but I managed to avoid the war. And I came here. I'd been hearing about...you know, what was going on; and I was very excited about it. I wanted to SEE..."socialism with a human face." I wanted to see it in action. And...uh...I was lucky. I immediately fell in with a group of people who were very welcoming. Who were...happy that I was here. Who spoke English! And...uh...had an idea of something they wanted to do—which was to create this journal. And I'd had some experience with that. I'd... *(Then)* So I joined in. And it was a very...very exciting time.

(ALISON is nodding, jotting down notes, seemingly distracted.)

ALISON: *(After a moment)* Now, you were...I mean, you're being a little bit modest. It wasn't like you joined a group that was already operating. You...it was when you got here that the journal actually happened. Right?

BARRY: *(Nodding, sheepish)* That's... I mean, they already had an idea, but...I think it's fair to say that it didn't start until we were all together. That's true.

ALISON: Until you showed them how.

BARRY: I wouldn't say that.

ALISON: Well. *(She smiles. Then)* Now the journal... I've managed to get a hold of some of the copies, but the journal was...how would you describe it exactly?

BARRY: It was a literary journal. *(Then)* Of course, at that time nothing was simply one thing. It was...and actually, it wasn't even purely literary. We published manifestos, we had political statements. Calls for political parties. *(Then)* But it was primarily literary.

ALISON: But subversive?

BARRY: Pardon?

ALISON: Its intention was subversive.

(BARRY chuckles, amused.)

BARRY: Yes.

(ALISON *hears how naive she just sounded.*)

ALISON: *(After a moment)* Now, this is '68. You published throughout the year—

BARRY: We published until 1970.

ALISON: *(Intrigued)* At which time...?

BARRY: *(Off-guard)* Pardon?

ALISON: What happened in 1970?

(BARRY *seems suddenly uneasy.*)

BARRY: We stopped.

(ALISON *nods, waiting for him to continue.*)

ALISON: Could you talk about that? What...? The reasons?

(BARRY *stares at her.*)

BARRY: The Russians.

ALISON: Well, I know, but...how did it come about?

(BARRY *looks away, growing more and more uncomfortable.*)

BARRY: Uh... *(Finally)* ...there were, uh...events—

ALISON: I... *(Immediate)* ...excuse me, I...actually know some of what happened. You were...I mean, correct me if I'm wrong, but you were stopped. Weren't you? At the border.

(BARRY *looks stricken.*)

BARRY: How do you know that?

ALISON: Well, there were...articles written.

BARRY: *(Edgy)* Saying what?

ALISON: Just...that. *(Beat)* That you were stopped. And that after you were stopped, people were arrested.

BARRY: That's a lie.

ALISON: People weren't arrested.

BARRY: Not because of me.

ALISON: Well—

BARRY: What articles?

ALISON: *(Off-guard)* What?

BARRY: *(Aggressive)* You say you read articles.
What articles?

ALISON: German, Swiss. There was something in
Der Spiegel, I remember.

BARRY: Well, they were lies! *(This last he practically
spits out.)*

BARRY: *(Then)* I wasn't...the situation was complicated,
but I was not responsible for anyone's arrest.

(Beat)

ALISON: Well, perhaps—

BARRY: Look, I... *(Shifting tacks)* I'm sorry. I didn't
realize we were going to be talking about this.

ALISON: Well, we won't... *(Easing up)* ...if you're not
comfortable.

BARRY: It's just...it was complicated. And I'd rather not
go into it.

ALISON: *(Careful)* I understand.

(Beat)

ALISON: So after you were stopped—

BARRY: I'm sorry, I...think maybe we should stop.

ALISON: *(Disappointed)* Really?

BARRY: I just—

ALISON: I'm happy to talk about today if you prefer.

BARRY: Maybe some other time.

(With that, BARRY stands. Once he does, ALISON watches him for a long moment. Then, realizing that he is determined, she reaches for her tape recorder.)

ALISON: You know, I feel terrible. I just...I had no intention of making you...of putting you on the spot. *(A beat)* Will you accept my apology?

BARRY: *(After a pause)* Of course.

ALISON: It's just that you're so important to us. Barry Axelrod! I mean, when I told everyone that I was interviewing you, that I had a story about you...you should have seen their faces. You are such a hero to us.

(Pause. BARRY is unmoved.)

ALISON: Do you believe me?

BARRY: I find it hard to believe. *(Then)* But yes, if you say so.

ALISON: Your commitment to this culture, to its people, to freedom...it's what we all emulate. Especially at my newspaper. We think about your example all the time. And that's why the idea of telling your story, of telling it in all its complexity...is so important to us. *(She takes a moment)* Please give me another chance.

(She looks at BARRY and for a long moment he doesn't respond. Then, finally...)

BARRY: Do you understand what I mean when I say it was complicated?

ALISON: Yes. I think so.

BARRY: I don't think you do.

(There is a long pause.)

BARRY: Truth is elusive. What people say, *why* they say it...those are complicated balances. You have to understand the people, their biases. You have to *know*...why they said what they said. If you weren't there, if you simply look back from today, in black and white terms...you're bound to misinterpret.

ALISON: So the only people who can discuss this, who can write about it, are those who experienced it.

BARRY: Those are the people who will write about it most intelligently, yes.

ALISON: But others will write about it, Barry. And someone like you will suffer. *(Continuing, picking up speed)* If your story isn't told, and told soon, you will suffer exactly the same fate that you say you most fear. At least with me you'll know you have someone who cares about you, who is sympathetic. Because Mister Axelrod, I have to tell you, I think what you've done here is incredible. I think your journalism center is...amazing. The fact that you're...you're bringing people a free press. That's incredible! But you're not going to get the credit you deserve if you don't talk about your past. And I would think you would rather talk about it with someone who is sympathetic to you...rather than someone who is not.

(Slight pause)

BARRY: Well, you would think wrong.

ALISON: Mister Axelrod—

BARRY: May I...stop you for a second? And ask you a question?

ALISON: *(Beat)* Certainly.

BARRY: Why should I trust you?

ALISON: *(Thrown)* Because... *(At a loss)* ...because—

BARRY: You see that's the thing. I *have* no reason to trust you.

ALISON: But you have no reason to trust anyone else. And what I'm saying is someone is going to write about this. At least with me you're getting a person who wants to write fairly. Who will give you the benefit of the doubt. *(Slight pause, persuasive)* Who will listen to your story.

(BARRY looks at her for a long moment.)

BARRY: *(Then, finally)* All right.

ALISON: You'll do it?

BARRY: On one condition.

ALISON: What?

BARRY: You work for me.

ALISON: *(Beat)* What??

BARRY: Come work for me. Come to my paper.

ALISON: You're joking.

BARRY: Not at all.

ALISON: How can I write my story if I'm working for you?

BARRY: It's the only way I'll consider it. And Alison, look, be serious. Where you work now is a joke. It'll close in six months. Come work for me and in six months time I'll have you back in New York with a job at *The Times*. That's a promise.

(ALISON is clearly tempted.)

ALISON: Tell me your story and I'll consider it.

BARRY: Consider it...and in time I will tell you my story. *(Beat)* Your choice.

(Holding her gaze for a moment, he then starts for the door.)

ALISON: Wait a minute! *(Beat)* Why did you stop? You let me get so far and then you stopped. Why?

BARRY: I made a mistake to start.

ALISON: Did you carry a list?

BARRY: I did...no, I... *(Enraged)* ...look, I said we should stop!

ALISON: Barry, three hundred people were arrested.

BARRY: Not because of me.

ALISON: Your name was connected to them.

BARRY: By the Communists! The Communists connected my name to them and you choose to believe them? *(This last he practically shrieks he is so angry.)*

ALISON: Tell me your story. Set the record straight.

BARRY: It's too complicated.

ALISON: Barry—

BARRY: Alison, I can't tell you in one or two sentences! But this I can tell you. I have enemies. And over the years they have said things about me, planted stories about me, that form the basis for your questions, and they are lies! *(He then continues, genuinely outraged.)* So let me set the record straight. I did not sell people out. I did not set people up. If anything, it was the other way around.

(The two stare at each other, BARRY *truly furious)*

BARRY: Now, please. *(With that, he then points to the door.)*

ALISON: I'll take it.

BARRY: Take what?

ALISON: The job.

BARRY: No. I don't think so.

ALISON: Barry, I believe you! I wouldn't take it if I didn't.

(At this, BARRY stares at her, a long moment passing.)

BARRY: Call me in the morning.

ALISON: Barry—

BARRY: I said...call me in the morning.

(And with that, he once again crosses to the door. Once he gets there, he holds it open—waiting for her. And finally, she comes.)

BARRY: And next time ask me if you can call me Barry.

ALISON: *(Beat)* I believe you.

(With that, she watches him for a moment to see if he'll answer. Then, when he doesn't—and it's clear that he won't—she exits.)

(Blackout. End Scene Two)

Scene Three

(The sitting room of a Germanic hunting lodge. Dominated by an elaborate array of mounted antlers, the room below is filled with a hodge-podge of antique furniture and wooden moving crates. And there in the center, on a couch the size of a small boat, sits MAREK—nervously waiting for someone to enter. When she does, it is DIANE.)

DIANE: Has he been in yet?

(MAREK turns, surprised, and stands. He is angry.)

MAREK: He has not, no. I...I—

DIANE: Are you all right?

MAREK: I would like you to get him, please.

DIANE: I... *(She looks over her shoulder)* ...um...I think he'll be right out.

MAREK: Please. I do not have time to wait.

DIANE: I think he's on the phone. *(She moves down the stairs.)* But I'm sure he'll be right out. I told him you were here. *(She smiles.)* Can I get you a drink?

MAREK: No. Thank you.

(Suddenly her face changes, looking for a moment quite serious.)

DIANE: Listen, I...want to apologize again about last night. I don't know what happened.

(MAREK looks away.)

DIANE: Will you forgive me?

MAREK: Yes.

(And with that, she again smiles. She then asks, immediately...)

DIANE: So when did you leave?

MAREK: Pardon?

DIANE: Last night. Did you stay long?

MAREK: No. Not long.

DIANE: Did you go back in?

MAREK: Did..?

DIANE: To the ballroom. *(Beat)* Did you go back in and dance?

MAREK: Oh. No, I...

DIANE: You *don't* forgive me, do you?

MAREK: *(Angry)* Please. I am not—

DIANE: I wish you would. I—

MAREK: *(Blurting)* I am not here to forgive you.
That is not why I've come!

DIANE: *(Beat, hurt)* I know.

MAREK: I am here for your husband. To see your
husband. I... *(He takes a deep breath, trying to control
himself.)* I am sorry. I don't... *(Rubbing his forehead)*
...please.

(Slight pause)

DIANE: Would you like me to leave?

MAREK: It is only that I am... *(He stops, caught in the
awkwardness.)* No. Please. *(Beat)* We should talk.

DIANE: About?

MAREK: *(Gritting his teeth)* What you would like.

DIANE: What would I like?

MAREK: *(Sharp)* Whatever you would like!

DIANE: You. *(This last she says disarmingly.)* I'd like to
talk about you.

MAREK: *(Beat, squirming even more)* What would you
like to know?

DIANE: Everything. *(Then, suddenly)* But first I'll find
Lubo. I'm sure he'd like to know, too. *(And with that,
she springs to her feet, returning to the landing.)*

DIANE: You sure I can't get you anything?

MAREK: No. Thank you. I—

DIANE: *(Turning, surprised)* Oh, God, there you are.
I was just coming to get you.

(LUBO appears on the landing from the hall.)

LUBO: I am sorry, Pavel. I had three lines at once.

*(MAREK stands as LUBO comes toward him, his hand
outstretched.)*

LUBO: What is this, Diana? He has nothing to drink.

DIANE: He said he was...on the job.

LUBO: *(To* MAREK*)* Is that what you said? That you were on the job?

MAREK: *(Confused)* I...

LUBO: That is not possible. When you come to my house, that is not possible. Here, Diana, please, bring us something!

*(*DIANE *leaves. As she does,* LUBO *holds up a finger indicating that* MAREK *should remain silent.)*

LUBO: I wanted us to have a second. Alone. She is beautiful, isn't she?

MAREK: *(Beat, then)* Your wife? Yes!

LUBO: No, not my wife. Separate from my wife. As a woman, alone, in the world; she is beautiful. Don't you think?

MAREK: *(Cautious)* I...

LUBO: You can say that. I don't... *(He puffs up.)* I take pride.

MAREK: She is beautiful, yes.

(A dangerous pause. LUBO *stares at him.)*

LUBO: And yet, and this is equally true, she is not happy. How is that possible? Explain that to me. How is it possible for a beautiful woman, in a marriage with a wealthy man, living in a palace for a house, not to be happy? How can that be?

MAREK: I am not married. I—

LUBO: Still, you must have an idea. You must know women. You must know the world. After all, you are the mayor of a city. You are a worldly man. How is that possible?

MAREK: *(Beat)* I—

LUBO: I have the answer. I will tell you. *(He touches both fingers to his head.)* The imagination...is not there. The imagination for happiness. *(He nods, knowingly)* I have been to...oh, seventy countries. Some of the poorest in the world. With people dying everywhere. Every day. And in the middle of pain...death...hunger, I have seen children smile and laugh...and play. I have seen some of the happiest people, with the most joy in their eyes, in the most terrible places. Because they had the imagination... *(Again he taps his head.)* ...they could see themselves in love. In pleasure. With hope. *(He smiles.)* It's true. *(He laughs.)* It's funny, isn't it? To you, as a mayor, I am sure it is very funny. Imagine if you should tell this to your people. "Don't...please...do not worry... how your life is. Imagine you are happy. And it shall be so." *(Again he laughs.)* You would be mayor for one day! *(Laughing harder)* Am I right?

MAREK: *(Laughing slightly)* Yes. I think.

LUBO: Because your people...why? What is it your people want?

(MAREK shakes his head, laughing still.)

LUBO: No, tell me, please. What is it they want?

MAREK: I—

LUBO: Magic! *(Slight pause)* Right now, especially, they want magic. "Tell us please, Mister Mayor, that we shall be safe from worry. From want. From the Russians. Assure us"...of something that no man can assure anybody of..."Assure us of tomorrow." *(Beat)* Am I wrong?

MAREK: It's...in our country right now it is very difficult.

LUBO: Which is why you and I are meant for each other.

(Just then DIANE appears on the landing.)

LUBO: Ah, back already. What did you bring us?

DIANE: Well, I know it's a little early yet, but I thought you all might like a drop of spirits. Mister Marek, you enjoyed this last night, didn't you?

MAREK: *(Uncertain)* I...

DIANE: Our whiskey. Our American whiskey. You told me last night you enjoyed it.

MAREK: Yes. I—

DIANE: And I thought you might like something from your side as well. *(She holds up a bottle of vodka.)* Lubo's favorite.

MAREK: No, I am sorry. It is too early yet.

DIANE: Oh, come on now. Don't say that.

MAREK: I—

DIANE: Look, you're stayin' for dinner, aren't you?

MAREK: I...don't think so.

DIANE: Of course, you are.

MAREK: No. I—

DIANE: Lubo, are you listening to this?

LUBO: Pavel, how can this be?

MAREK: I am sorry, Mister Brodsky, I—

LUBO: *(Aggressive)* Why you must go? Huh? Why?

MAREK: I... *(Uncomfortable)* ...my people wait for me. I—

LUBO: *(Blustering)* So call them. Please. Go in the other room and call them. Tell them *not* to wait.

MAREK: It is not possible.

LUBO: It is not possible for you leave! *That* is not possible! Everything else is possible. *(Beat, seemingly heartfelt)* Pavel, please. It is important.

(Slight pause)

MAREK: All right. I will stay for dinner.

DIANE: *(Exuberant)* And if you're stayin' for dinner, you're stayin' for drinks. What'll it be?

MAREK: The vodka. I will have... *(He gestures a small glass)* ...not much.

(DIANE pours happily.)

DIANE: You know, I was telling Lubo the other day, there's nothing I like more than seeing a man with his vodka. That's...we don't have enough of that anymore. *(Having passed out the drinks, she holds hers aloft.)*

DIANE: So...

LUBO: Let's let Pavel make the toast. To what do we drink, Pavel?

MAREK: *(Awkward, embarrassed)* As always, to friendship.

LUBO: Ah! To friendship!

(LUBO immediately downs his glass, followed quickly by DIANE. MAREK merely sips.)

LUBO: You know, I was telling to Diane, when we were thinking of coming here, the one thing—and this is different from Czechs in America—the one thing you will notice in my country is the friendliness of the people. There are no people in the world more friendly than Czechs. And it's true. I tell you that from the bottom of my heart, it's true. *(He turns, quickly)* Do you think so, Diana? What do you think?

DIANE: It's true.

LUBO: Has this not been the case? Since we were here?

DIANE: It has.

(Slight pause)

LUBO: Certainly it has. And you know the proof of it? Right here with you. Here we are talking and not letting you say a word. Pavel, please, tell us about yourself.

MAREK: About—

LUBO: Who you are. Where you're from. Actually though, before you begin... *(He reaches for the bottle.)*

MAREK: No, please. I—

LUBO: Pavel, please, where are you going?

MAREK: Nowhere, I—

LUBO: So then what is the harm?

MAREK: I am sorry. I don't...drink so much, I—

LUBO: Pavel, please. If anything should happen I will carry you. On my back. To my room. *(Beat)* Please.

MAREK: *(Finally, relenting)* All right.

LUBO: There you are! *(He pours triumphantly.)*

LUBO: So. Then. You were saying.

MAREK: Please?

LUBO: You were saying. About yourself, your family?

MAREK: No, I—

LUBO: Actually, something I have been wondering. You are mayor here, yes?

MAREK: Yes.

LUBO: How did that happen? How did a man such as you become mayor?

MAREK: Why, I am not qualified?

LUBO: Oh, no. You are more than qualified. A man of great wisdom, I think. But mayors and wisdom, they don't always go together.

MAREK: That's true.

LUBO: So?

(Beat)

MAREK: Well, actually it's funny story. My friend...how do you say it...from childhood...was going to be mayor, and he called me. I was in Prague, and he asked me if I would come to be assistant to him. Assistant mayor. And I said yes. But then...when I came he did not want to be mayor anymore. So...I became mayor.

DIANE: He changed his mind.

MAREK: Yes.

LUBO: *(Quick)* And?

MAREK: Please?

LUBO: You made the right decision? You're happy?

MAREK: Ah...happy. Who knows?

LUBO: It is not good if you're not happy.

MAREK: Well... *(Shrugging)* ...some days I am happy.

DIANE: That's—

LUBO: "Some days" is not good enough, Pavel. You must be happy every day.

MAREK: Then—

LUBO: And I can make it so. *(Beat, eyes twinkling)* If you will let me.

MAREK: *(Beat, confused)* You—

LUBO: *(Quick, commanding)* Reach down.

MAREK: *(Confused)* Reach..?

LUBO: Down. Beneath your seat.

(MAREK reaches, uncertain.)

LUBO: Under.

DIANE: Lubo—

LUBO: Diana!

(LUBO *watches as* MAREK *finally removes a thin, spiral notebook from beneath his seat, placing it in his lap.*)

LUBO: *(Then, seductively)* Right now, and in the future also, you will have many people approach you. And each will tell you a story. They will come from Germany, Austria...others from America maybe, and the story will always be the same. How you can make miracles. How you can take this tiny town of yours and turn it into the jewel of Bohemia. *(Slight beat)* This story will always be the same. A fairy tale. *That* story... *(He points.)* ...the story in that book...is not.

MAREK: *(Beat, awed)* What is it?

LUBO: Read. Side one is English, side two is Czech.

(MAREK *opens the book.*)

DIANE: That—

LUBO: *(Sharp)* Diana!

DIANE: *(Beat, fearful)* What?

(*He holds up his hand.*)

LUBO: Please.

(*He then watches as* MAREK *reads.*)

LUBO: Do you know what is alchemy, Pavel?

MAREK: *(Looking up, distracted)* What is..?

LUBO: Alchemy. *(Beat)* From the Middle Ages. Alchemy.

MAREK: Alch—

LUBO: The science of kings.

MAREK: *(Still confused)* Oh. Yes.

LUBO: Everywhere...from lead into gold.

(Beat)

MAREK: I don't understand.

LUBO: You have eight kilometers from here a mountaintop filled with lead. Horrible on the outside, rising into the sky, it contains within it enough hot gas and molten lava to burn and torture the people of not only your country...but several beyond. And these people worry, Pavel. They think only of that gas, that lava. They don't realize...it can also be gold. *(Pause)* Your job, so near to this dangerous, beautiful mountaintop is to open their eyes to it. Let them see beyond what they fear. Let them find what they hope. *(Beat)* And I can help you do that.

MAREK: *(Confused)* I signed a paper.

LUBO: I know.

MAREK: I am... *(Beat)* ...this is Temelin you are talking about?

LUBO: Yes.

MAREK: I am against it!

LUBO: I know.

(Slight pause)

MAREK: I don't understand.

LUBO: Read the book.

MAREK: *(With growing alarm)* Is this why I am meeting with you? Because of Temelin?

LUBO: Temelin is the mountaintop.

MAREK: I cannot be convinced! *(He puts down the book on the table.)*

LUBO: Pavel, tell me something. This paper you signed? You were alone?

MAREK: *(Combative)* Not at all. There were others.

LUBO: How many?

MAREK: One hundred!

LUBO: And all of them mayors?

MAREK: All of them mayors, yes. A hundred mayors throughout this entire region who do not want for us here nuclear power!

LUBO: And yet it will open. Won't it? *(His tone aggressive)* This plant. Eventually.

MAREK: *(Grudging)* Eventually, yes. I suppose.

LUBO: And how will your people benefit, Pavel? When this plant has opened and our bid is accepted...how will your people benefit?

(Slight pause)

MAREK: I must do what I think is right. If I do that, my people will understand. And benefit.

(The two men stare at each other a long moment.)

LUBO: I know what you are thinking. Already you think you know me. Yes? That I am the devil.

(MAREK nods, almost imperceptibly.)

LUBO: Do you know who else thinks that? *(His voice starting to rise)* Every other group who burn with the certainty that God alone has talked to them! *(He seems barely under control now.)* My uncle, Pavel, talked like that when he spoke of the bourgeoisie, the aristocracy— how the workers would beat the truth out of those who would lie to them. *(Beat)* And now you do the same.

MAREK: I am not like that.

LUBO: Pavel, listen to me. I have not come to this town, to this region, because I am a stranger here. I come because I was born in Karlovec! I was born not two kilometers from this mountain we are speaking of. *(His voice again starting to rise)* And I have not come to the land of my birth, to this place that I loved as a child, to watch it sink back into the madness and stupidity it just barely escaped from. *(Beat, gathering himself)* But I have not come home to hurt you, either. I have not come home, to *make this* my home...so that I might poison the ground that I walk on. I have come with a plan, to make this town, this whole region, better. And all I ask is that you read it. *(Beat)* Will you do that? Will you read it?

(Pause)

MAREK: *(Finally, grudging)* Yes.

(Slight pause)

LUBO: Good. *(Suddenly he stands, smiling.)* Then enough of that now. We'll have plenty of time for talking and arguing. Let's eat. *(To* DIANE*)* Can we eat?

DIANE: Yes. *(She stands too)* I... It'll just take me a minute.

(She exits. As soon as she does LUBO *laughs.)*

LUBO: Did you see her face?

MAREK: What?

LUBO: When we were talking just now, did you see her face? She had no idea we were playing. She thought we were serious. This is why women should never be in politics. *(He says this last with a wink)* They have no feel for nuance.

(By now on the platform, he gestures for MAREK *to join him.)*

LUBO: Come. I will show you the sauna.

(And soon, MAREK *and* LUBO *are gone.)*

(End Scene Three)

Scene Four

(BARRY's *office.* ALISON *is again at the circular table, while* BARRY, *not far from her, is staring out a window.* ALISON *waits patiently, her attention rapt. Finally, he speaks.)*

BARRY: I have a story that could blow the roof off this country. If it does, it will wind up in every paper in the world. *(He turns to her.)* Wanna write it?

ALISON: *(Beat, breathless)* I'll listen.

(BARRY *comes to the table.)*

BARRY: Lubo Brodsky.

ALISON: What?

BARRY: Who. A person. Lubo Brodsky.

ALISON: What about him?

BARRY: He's a man I knew twenty years ago who until recently has been living in America.

ALISON: And?

BARRY: Three months ago he showed up at the Embassy. Within days of that, he was talking to the ministers of trade and energy.

ALISON: *(Perplexed)* I...still don't get it.

(BARRY's *eyes glisten with excitement.)*

BARRY: He's been working for a company called C D I. A company I'd never heard of so I looked into it. What I found was a phone number in Philadelphia connected to an office in Maryland. But not just any office. An office missing a desk. And not just any town. Fort Meade. The home of army intelligence.

ALISON: Meaning...what?

BARRY: Meaning what do you think?

ALISON: He's a spy?

BARRY: He isn't a tourist.

ALISON: *(Beat)* And? What does he want?

BARRY: Something to do with Temelin.

ALISON: With..?

BARRY: Temelin.

ALISON: I—

BARRY: You don't know Temelin?

(ALISON *starts to shake her head, only to have* BARRY *immediately continue.*)

BARRY: It's the Soviet nuclear plant built in the eighties that has yet to go on line. But because it's near Austria it's not *going* to go on line until it's been renovated. Which is where Mister Brodsky steps in. There are currently three different companies, one of them Westinghouse, doing the bidding on this work; work that can lead to other similar work throughout Eastern Europe. Because Temelin, you see, is not alone out there. There are literally dozens of other plants, all built by the Soviets and all needing face lifts, that are dotting the landscape. If they can figure out how to do this one; if they can figure out how to fuel it and cool it and store all the waste; they can make billions, and I mean *billions* of dollars in contracts.

(ALISON *stares at* BARRY, *breathless.*)

ALISON: And the story is...what exactly?

BARRY: Who knows? Right now Brodsky's in Karlovec, a town down there, talking to the Mayor. Only I don't think he's just talking. I think he's bribing everyone he can get his hands on. I think... (*He thinks better of it.*) ...who knows what the story is?

(Beat)

ALISON: And you know this all...how?

BARRY: I have a friend in the Ministry who isn't pleased.

ALISON: So why doesn't he do something?

BARRY: Because Brodsky also has friends—and they *are* pleased.

(Again she stares at him.)

ALISON: And you know him...how?

BARRY: Who?

ALISON: Brodsky. You said you knew him once. How?

(And now it's BARRY who stares back at her.)

BARRY: *(Then)* He was my partner. *(Pause)* It was he I started the journal with.

(And with that, ALISON reacts—as if a tumbler has fallen.)

ALISON: I see. And—

BARRY: Alison. *(This last a bit sharp)* Not now. Don't ask any more now.

(She stares at him.)

ALISON: *(Then)* O K.

BARRY: You'll do it?

ALISON: Yes.

BARRY: Good.

ALISON: On one condition.

BARRY: What?

ALISON: You tell me why you changed your mind.

BARRY: I didn't.

ALISON: You did. When I left your office the other day you were through with me. Now you've asked me back.

BARRY: You misunderstood.

ALISON: You weren't angry?

BARRY: I was furious. But that's not the point. What I was more than anything was intrigued. I knew I had found a writer I wanted to work with and that's what I focussed on afterwards.

(Slight pause)

ALISON: When do I start?

BARRY: Tomorrow. Morning. Come to my office and we'll arrange everything then.

ALISON: *(Suddenly, blurting)* I'm still writing you, you know. Just because I'm doing this doesn't mean I'm not writing you.

BARRY: *(Even)* All right.

(Beat)

ALISON: All right what?

BARRY: All right, I understand.

ALISON: You'll help me?

BARRY: Yes. I'll... *(Then)* ...yes.

(She watches him.)

ALISON: *(On edge)* I've collected my notes. They're all with a friend.

BARRY: Fine. *(Then)* I—

ALISON: Why did they stop you?

BARRY: What?

ALISON: You were stopped, at the border, why?

BARRY: I wasn't stopped!

ALISON: You never—

BARRY: *(Enraged)* Alison, look, I said I would help you and I will. But don't play me!

ALISON: *(Pushing, edgy)* Barry, I'm not alone on this. There are others out there who know this as well.

BARRY: Are you threatening me?

ALISON: I'm just saying that sooner or later you're going to have to tell it. Why not tell it to me?

BARRY: I'll tell you what—

ALISON: First tell me this. Did you leave on your own or were you asked?

BARRY: I was asked. *(Immediate)* Listen to me. *(Furious)* As much as I don't understand it, there are clearly people out there who think my story is important. And so you're right, I *am* going to have to tell it. But... *(He holds up his finger.)* ...I don't want to be played. I will tell you my story on my terms at my time. If that's satisfactory to you, fine. If not, and you continue to push, I'll give it to somebody else.

(A short beat)

ALISON: *(Then, continuing to push)* Just tell me this. Why Salzburg?

BARRY: *(Annoyed)* What?

ALISON: You left here and went there. Why?

BARRY: I—

ALISON: Why didn't you go home?

BARRY: Because this *is* my home. And if I couldn't stay here, I wanted to stay close.

ALISON: For what reason?

BARRY: *(Thrown)* I—

ALISON: Did you think you could come back?

BARRY: I hoped so, yes.

ALISON: Did you have reason to hope?

(BARRY *eyes her furiously.*)

BARRY: What are you implying?

ALISON: I'm just asking.

BARRY: It sounds like you're implying something.

ALISON: I'm just asking, Barry. Did you have reason to hope? Because most people didn't. Most people left here and went home. They didn't stay in the region.

(*Their eyes now locked on each other,* BARRY *responds bitterly.*)

BARRY: And I did.

ALISON: Yes.

BARRY: Why?

ALISON: (*Nodding*) That's...what I'm asking.

BARRY: Because I was in love. Because I was twenty-four and I was in love.

ALISON: With Sarka Rebanova?

BARRY: (*Shocked*) What?

ALISON: Is that who you were in love with?

(BARRY *is stunned.*)

BARRY: How did you know that?

ALISON: You'd be surprised what I know.

(BARRY *stares at her, clearly unnerved.*)

BARRY: Yes. Sarka Rebanova. And I wanted to stay nearby. I... (*Rattled*) ...I thought maybe she could get out.

ALISON: But she didn't.

BARRY: No. (*Then*) She didn't.

(A moment then passes as ALISON *continues to study him in silence—then suddenly she stands.)*

ALISON: All right.

BARRY: All right what?

ALISON: All right, I'll see you tomorrow.

BARRY: *(Panicking)* Where are you going?

ALISON: Home.

BARRY: Alison!

(He stops her. She turns back.)

BARRY: May I walk you?

ALISON: No. *(Beat)* Thanks. *(Beat)* I'll take the bus.

(And with that, she exits, as BARRY *continues to stare after her—and the lights slowly fade to black.)*

(End Scene Four)

Scene Five

(The hunting lodge. From offstage we hear the sounds of an argument as MAREK *and* LUBO *approach.)*

MAREK: *(Off)* I'm sorry...I think I have made a terrible mistake.

LUBO: *(Off, anxiously)* What mistake, what?

MAREK: *(Off)* My town...I think...

*(*LUBO *enters in front of* MAREK, *gesturing for him to follow.)*

LUBO: Come in, sit, please.

MAREK: No. I—

LUBO: Pavel, please.

MAREK: No! *(Then, hearing himself shouting, he quiets.)*
I mean...I am sorry, I...I think that is the problem.

(By now the two men are facing each other. And LUBO *sees how nervous and at the same time determined* MAREK's *become.)*

LUBO: I see.

MAREK: Please, I—

LUBO: Can I get you a drink?

MAREK: No! I...must leave soon. *(Then)* But I want to tell you...why it is not possible. Your plan.

(With this, he hands back LUBO's *notebook.)*

MAREK: Your book.

LUBO: Pavel—

MAREK: Please let me talk. *(Then, again, for emphasis)*
Please let me talk. *(He then laughs, suddenly, in embarrassment.)* I had everything in my head and now I... *(Then)* This is a small town. As you know.
And the people, we are not...we do not have the perfect idea. *I* do not have the perfect idea. But I have some idea. We can not be jewel of Bohemia. It is wrong for us to try. Let other people, other towns, be jewels.
For us, here, I would like to be normal. To be a normal European town. You see, you in America, that is...
you don't think about that. You *are* normal. You are always normal. You have not had forty years...where...
(Becoming upset, he calms himself.) ...but we have. And so to build a cinema maybe, a park, to line the streets with trees, for Communists this is not useful. For human beings it is. And so that is what I want.

LUBO: *(Eager)* And we can do that.

MAREK: *(Off-guard)* I—

LUBO: Did you read the book?

MAREK: Yes.

LUBO: Did you read what was in the book?

MAREK: I did. But—

LUBO: We can do that, Pavel. We can do all of that.

MAREK: But not the way I want! I don't want...I don't
want a park to decorate a nuclear plant. I don't want...
(Furious now) ...I don't want to put lipstick on a whore!
(Then, regretting how he's said it) I am sorry, I... I do not
mean to say that.

LUBO: Pavel—

MAREK: Let me finish. I don't want anymore to think
big. To think of the sweep of history. Of a bright and
brilliant future. These are the words of Communism.
These are the promises that had us enslaved. Because
it was so big and so bright and so beautiful, we must of
course be willing to sacrifice. And so that's all we did.
For forty years we sacrificed and I am tired of it. I don't
want to sacrifice anymore. I don't want to think big.
I want to think small. I want for every human being
to have enough. *(Beat)* That's all.

LUBO: You know what you really want? To be a hero.

MAREK: No.

LUBO: Yes. I hear it in your voice.

MAREK: No—

LUBO: Yes. That is what you're doing, you see. You talk
to me here, you make a speech to me here, I hear it in
the Parliament. *You* can hear it in the Parliament. *(His
tone mocking)* You are seeing yourself on the floor of the
Parliament and you are making this speech and people
are getting to their feet, with tears in their eyes, they are
clapping their hands, and you are their hero. *You* are
their *hero!*

MAREK: *(Wounded)* That is not—

LUBO: But it is not so. You are not their hero. They are not getting to their feet. You know what they are doing? Asking you questions. *(In rapid succession)* "Mister Marek, please, tell us, what of this hospital? Is it true there was a hospital? That they offered a hospital? Is it true, Mister Marek?" And what will you say?

MAREK: *(Uncomfortable)* I will say...

LUBO: *(Aggressive)* What?

MAREK: *(Faltering)* ...that...

LUBO: You will talk to them, of course. Please tell me you will talk to them.

(MAREK shifts in his seat, suddenly nervous.)

LUBO: Oh Pavel, you must. Do you understand that you must? That in a democracy you must?

MAREK: *(Weakly)* Yes.

LUBO: But you don't want to, do you? You don't want to talk to them and tell them what we offered. Do you?

MAREK: No.

LUBO: Why?

MAREK: I—

LUBO: Because they will not agree with you, will they? They will take our offer. Won't they?

MAREK: They will be tempted. Yes.

(LUBO laughs, bitterly.)

LUBO: They will be tempted.

MAREK: For us—

LUBO: Pavel, do you know who you sound like? The way you refer to them? "They will be tempted." A Communist. Talking about the masses. "They will

be tempted." And so you must protect them, yes?
Is that what you're doing? Are you protecting them,
Pavel? From themselves?

(MAREK *is speechless,* LUBO's *attack having cut him to the
quick.*)

MAREK: *(Finally)* I... *(Then)* ...what you say... *(Again he
gathers himself)* Our country right now is very poor.
We...have not...there are many things we need. The
things your company offers...in this book...we need.
But we do not need for our children to die, or our
grandchildren...when you are gone, when your hospital
has crumbled, when your apartment buildings are
falling down...and the radiation from your plant goes
into our water.

LUBO: *(Sharp)* What are you talking about?

MAREK: I—

LUBO: What are you talking about, "goes into your
water?" What are you talking about?

MAREK: I am saying—

LUBO: That is bullshit, what you are saying. "Goes into
the water." That is bullshit!

MAREK: Before I came here I was engineer. Nuclear
engineer. I know what I am talking about.

(LUBO *is stunned. And for a moment, he is stuck.*)

LUBO: All right, look, you don't, but I will not argue.
I will simply ask you. Put it to the people. See what they
say. Will you do that?

MAREK: I...

LUBO: Pavel, if you don't, I will. I will put it to one of
your enemies. Vacha, for instance, this man Vacha. And
let him take it to the people. Would you prefer that?

(This last he says harshly as MAREK *stares back at him in silence.)*

LUBO: Pavel, listen to me. You are a good man. I know you are a good man. But your ideas about this plant are wrong. Let me prove it to you. May I prove it to you?

*(*MAREK *continues to stare.)*

LUBO: Or here, how 'bout this? I will have a study sent. From my office, I will have a study. I will show you how safe it is. This plant of ours. Our plans. May I send it to you?

*(*MAREK *nods his head slightly.)*

LUBO: You see, we don't have to...this does not have to be settled today. I want only for you to keep open your mind. That's all. Will you keep open your mind?

(Again MAREK *nods. Meanwhile, above them both,* DIANE *has appeared on the landing.)*

DIANE: *(Without pause)* Lubo.

LUBO: Not now.

DIANE: There is someone to see you.

LUBO: I said "not now"!

DIANE: From the Congress.

(This stops him.)

LUBO: What Congress?

DIANE: The American Congress.

LUBO: To see me?

DIANE: Yes.

LUBO: What does he want?

DIANE: She. Wouldn't say. Just...to see you.

(At this, MAREK *stands.)*

MAREK: Perhaps I should—

LUBO: No, please, I'll...

(*As* LUBO *crosses to the landing, he waves* MAREK *back down.*)

DIANE: *(To* LUBO, *quietly)* With questions.

LUBO: What?

DIANE: She has questions. To ask.

LUBO: What kind of questions?

DIANE: About the plant.

(*By now* LUBO *is on the platform next to* DIANE. *He turns back to* MAREK.)

LUBO: I'll be back.

(*And with that, he exits. As soon as he does,* DIANE *wheels on* MAREK, *her tone when she speaks to him strident and whispered.*)

DIANE: *(Hissed)* I need to see you.

MAREK: *(Off-guard)* What?

DIANE: *(Louder)* I need to see you! It's urgent I see you!

MAREK: *(Hushing her)* Diana—

DIANE: Diane. My husband calls me Diana, my name is Diane!

MAREK: Diane—

DIANE: Pavel, don't argue with me. Just tell me you'll see me.

MAREK: *(Beat)* I—

DIANE: *(Sharp, scathing)* Are you afraid of him, Pavel? Is that it?

MAREK: *(On edge)* I am, yes!

DIANE: Good. You should be. He's a dangerous man. *(She starts down the stairs.)* Which is why you should see me.

MAREK: Diane—

DIANE: Pavel, listen to me. Don't talk. Just listen. *(By now she is next to him)* I know exactly what he wants from you. I will tell you what he wants. Just tell me that you'll see me.

MAREK: I—

DIANE: *(Desperate)* Tell me that you'll see me!

MAREK: *(Quick)* I'll see you.

DIANE: When?

MAREK: Tonight.

DIANE: Where?

MAREK: At...my weekend home. I have a weekend home. We can meet there.

DIANE: Good. Write down the directions. Leave them in the mailbox.

MAREK: What?

DIANE: Write down the directions. Leave them in the mailbox. Pavel, I know everything. I will tell you everything.

(Suddenly, she hears LUBO coming)

DIANE: Quick, step away.

(With that, she pushes MAREK away from her just as LUBO enters from the hallway. LUBO is excited.)

LUBO: You will never guess what just happened. *(He turns back to the hall.)* Miss Crawford?

(ALISON enters beside him.)

LUBO: This is Alison Crawford.

(With her hair pulled back and a new pair of jeans,
ALISON *has clearly made an effort to dress herself up.*
It is only moderately successful. She smiles, nervously,
as LUBO *steps into the living room.)*

LUBO: Alison, this is my wife, Diana.

ALISON: Hello.

(The two women shake hands.)

LUBO: And Pavel Marek...our Mayor here in Karlovec.

*(*MAREK *bows stiffly.)*

MAREK: Hello.

ALISON: *(To* MAREK*)* I am very glad to meet you.

*(*LUBO *continues, his tone exuberant, his smile wide.*
He also glances, meaningfully, at DIANE*.)*

LUBO: You will never guess what has happened.
Alison has just returned from the States and the
Congress has decided to support the loan guarantees.

DIANE: *(Playing along, excited)* Which...means what
exactly?

ALISON: *(Caught off-guard, surprised)* Actually, it's
not...decided yet...but it's leaning that way.

LUBO: *(Overlapping)* And she is here as fact-finder.

ALISON: Just to see that...everything is...the way it seems.

DIANE: *(Smiling)* How does it seem?

LUBO: Miss Crawford, please, sit down. *(He points to the*
couch.)

ALISON: *(Continuing)* Well, Mister Marek is here.
I assume...that means—

LUBO: *(Jumping in, to* MAREK*)* I told her you were here
and we were discussing environment.

*(*MAREK *is silent.)*

ALISON: And that... *(Cocking her head)* ...seems to be true. Isn't it?

(Slight pause)

MAREK: *(Finally)* Yes.

(Beat)

ALISON: *(Continuing, to* MAREK*)* And you're satisfied? You're—?

LUBO: You see, this is where you should take heart, Pavel. The Congress would not even consider such things if they did not have utter confidence. Isn't that right?

ALISON: *(Thrown)* Isn't..?

LUBO: Is the Congress not confident in us? In our industry?

ALISON: *(Uneasy)* It is, yes.

LUBO: This is especially the case since Three Mile Island. We have devoted...well, I know in the case of our company alone, we have devoted *millions* of dollars to studying safety. All mandated by the government. Yes?

ALISON: Yes.

LUBO: Have you read them? Are you...familiar?

ALISON: *(More uneasy)* I am, yes.

LUBO: And it is for that reason that the Congress is so interested, Pavel. Because it *is* so safe. Because American technology, and I say this with all... due modesty, is the best in the world. Isn't it?

ALISON: Yes.

*(*LUBO *smiles at her, then turns back to* MAREK.*)*

LUBO: So, you see...take heart. *(Then)* But look, enough of that now. We can have technical discussions all afternoon. In the meantime...let's have lunch.

MAREK: I can't.

LUBO: What do you mean?

MAREK: I must go. *(He stands.)* I have new meeting.

LUBO: Nonsense.

MAREK: No, it's true. I must go.

LUBO: That's—

ALISON: Actually, I'm sorry. I shouldn't have barged in on you like this.

LUBO: Of course, you should.

ALISON: *(Overlapping)* I should go, too.

LUBO: Nonsense.

DIANE: Lubo, let them go. If they have to go, let them go.

LUBO: I will do no such thing. Listen to me, both of you. I will not have you come into my house and then turn around and leave it. That simply isn't possible. Not to mention the fact that it hurts my feelings. Now, please—

MAREK: *(Immediate)* I can't.

LUBO: What do you mean?

MAREK: I—

LUBO: *(Harsh)* Pavel, who you are meeting with? Huh? Tell me that.

MAREK: My town council.

LUBO: At what time?

MAREK: At three.

LUBO: And now it is noon. It is just barely noon.

MAREK: Still—

LUBO: Are you embarrassed, Pavel? Has something embarrassed you?

MAREK: Not at all.

LUBO: Then why you must leave us?

MAREK: I said—

LUBO: You had a new meeting, I know. But now it is lunch time. There is no one who will meet you until three. At the earliest. Why you must go now?

MAREK: I simply must! *(This last he says a bit too forcefully. He then tries to recover.)*

MAREK: I am sorry.

(Beat)

LUBO: I see.

(Beat)

LUBO: All right, look, I'll tell you what I will do. Since it is clear that you don't want to be with us anymore, that you are embarrassed, I will make you a deal. What time will your meeting be over? Your town meeting?

MAREK: *(Beat, uneasy)* At five.

LUBO: Then call me then. Will you? *(Beat)* Will you do that? I want to continue our conversation. *(He leans in, his tone utterly reasonable.)* Will you do that?

(A moment passes.)

MAREK: *(Finally)* Yes.

(Beat. He smiles.)

LUBO: Good.

(With that, he then hands MAREK the notebook again— before turning, with a smile, to ALISON.)

LUBO: As for you—

ALISON: You know, I am really embarrassed. I mean, you talk about embarrassed, that's me.

LUBO: And why is that?

ALISON: I should have called first. I mean, I can't believe I came here without calling.

LUBO: Well—

ALISON: Here, I'll tell you what I'll do. I mean, if it's O K. I have a room in town, a hotel room, why don't I go there and check in? And then I'll come right back. I promise. *(Smiling, innocent)* Just give me a chance to freshen up.

DIANE: And me a chance to make lunch.

ALISON: Exactly.

(She turns back to LUBO.*)*

ALISON: Would that be all right?

*(*LUBO *regards her a moment.)*

LUBO: *(Suspicious)* If you like.

ALISON: My only problem is I need a ride.

LUBO: I'll drive you.

ALISON: Actually...is Mister Marek going to town?

LUBO: *(Beat)* That's—

ALISON: Perhaps...I can get a ride from him.

MAREK: *(Uneasy, but trapped)* Of course.

ALISON: And then...perhaps you can pick me up later.

(This last she says to LUBO.*)*

LUBO: *(Measured)* All right.

ALISON: Listen, I want to apologize again for being so...thoughtless. It won't happen again.

(By now she is shaking hands with LUBO.*)*

ALISON: I'll see you in an hour.

DIANE: I'll walk you out.

LUBO: Diana! *(This last comes out a bit sharply. He modulates his tone.)*

LUBO: I'm sorry, I... There is something we need to talk about. Would you come right back?

DIANE: *(Wary)* Of course. *(With that, she gestures to the others.)* This way.

(And soon the three exit. Once they have, LUBO *crosses to the window where he watches* ALISON *and* MAREK *leaving the house. he then waits for* DIANE *to return. Once she does, he speaks to her in a low, menacing voice.)*

LUBO: What are you doing?

DIANE: What?

LUBO: You're are doing something here. What?

DIANE: Nothing, I'm—

LUBO: *(Exploding, enraged)* DIANA, WHAT ARE YOU DOING!!!

DIANE: Nothing. *(Beat, terrified)* I don't know what you mean.

LUBO: *(Seething, intense)* I am sensing something I don't like. That I hope I am not right about. You are not confused, I hope, about your sympathies. *(Beat)* Are you? About where they lie?

DIANE: *(Meekly)* No.

(Beat)

LUBO: Good. *(Pause)* Because if you were...it would be very bad for you.

DIANE: *(Quiet)* I'm not.

LUBO: *(Beat, dangerous)* Good.

(With that, LUBO stares at her a long moment—making sure his point is made. He then starts for the stairway.)

DIANE: I'm seeing him.

LUBO: *(Annoyed)* What?

DIANE: Tonight. At his weekend home. I'm seeing him.

(This last brings a smile to LUBO's face.)

LUBO: Good again. *(He then starts up the stairway.)*

DIANE: Lubo.

(Only to have him stop once again.)

LUBO: What!

DIANE: Who is she?

(Beat. LUBO shakes his head.)

LUBO: I don't know. *(Then, looking offstage)* Not who she pretends. *(Then, back to DIANE)* But Diana, I am serious. Your problem is not with her. It is with me. Don't make a foolish mistake.

(Again LUBO takes a moment to make sure his point is made. he then exits. And DIANE is left alone on stage—as the lights, very slowly, fade to black.)

(End Scene Five)

END OF ACT ONE

ACT TWO

Scene Six

(LUBO and BARRY are facing the audience in two pools of light. LUBO is practically screaming, he is so upset. BARRY is unnerved. They are talking by phone.)

LUBO: Barry, you are doing something here. What are you doing?

BARRY: Nothing, I'm—

LUBO: *(Loud)* What are you doing, Barry!

BARRY: Nothing!

LUBO: Why is she here?

BARRY: Who?

LUBO: *(Sharp)* This girl. Alison.

BARRY: She's a reporter.

LUBO: And?

BARRY: I thought she could help us.

LUBO: In what way?

BARRY: She can find it.

LUBO: Find what?

BARRY: The check.

(There is an ominous silence.)

BARRY: Lubo, we need to find the check. If she finds it, we get him. *(Then)* Plus, Lubo, listen to me, I'll be down, too. I'll be down—

LUBO: Did you tell her about it?

BARRY: About?

LUBO: The check.

BARRY: No. I mean, not explicitly. I just said there was a pay-off, that I thought there was a pay-off. *(Beat)* Lubo, I'm telling you, it'll be better this way. *(Beat)* Plus, like I said, I'll be down, too. I'll be down tomorrow.

LUBO: *(Beat, then, angry, fast)* You know, Barry, I'm getting a feeling I don't like. Do you know what it is?

BARRY: No.

LUBO: It's the feeling of being fucked. I'm getting the feeling of being fucked, Barry. And I don't like it.

BARRY: Lubo—

LUBO: Barry, listen to me. Don't talk. Just listen. *(He takes a moment)* I remember most things in my life, but there is nothing I remember more clearly than a little bar in Prague called U Kralu. Do you remember U Kralu, Barry?

BARRY: Yes.

LUBO: Tell me about it.

BARRY: Lubo—

LUBO: Tell me about it, Barry!

BARRY: Lubo, I get the point!

(Beat)

LUBO: Do you know what would happen if I were to tell the people at the ministry or the lustration committee about U Kralu? About what happened there. Do you have any idea?

(There is a silence.)

LUBO: Well, I will tell you. They would kick you out in two seconds. In two seconds, this life you have built here, that you have struggled so hard to achieve, would be over. And you would return once again to the struggling, stupid... *(Practically spitting)* ...pathetic life you were living in Austria. Do you want that to happen, Barry? *(Beat, belligerent)* Huh? Do you want to work once again as a janitor?

BARRY: No.

(Beat)

LUBO: Then think very carefully about what you are doing here. And make sure you're not fucking me.

(Long pause)

BARRY: *(Quiet)* I will. *(Then, suddenly, pointed)* But Lubo! One thing to remember. I was not alone at U Kralu. You were there, too.

(Silence)

BARRY: *(Then)* I'll see you tomorrow.

(Blackout. End Scene Six)

Scene Seven

(MAREK's weekend house. MAREK stands at the counter making two cups of tea. He is wearing pajama bottoms. DIANE watches him from beneath the covers in bed).

DIANE: *(Even)* I wasn't wrong about you.

(Pause. MAREK looks her over.)

DIANE: *(Soft, sexy)* I knew from the first time I saw you you were different than you seemed.

MAREK: Different in what way?

DIANE: Stronger. In every way stronger.

(He turns to her, tray in hand.)

MAREK: I should be flattered.

(He crosses to her, extending the tray.)

DIANE: What's this?

MAREK: Tea.

(She shakes her head.)

DIANE: Beck.

MAREK: *(Not understanding)* Please?

DIANE: Becherovka. *(She gestures with her head.)* I prefer Beck.

(MAREK reaches for the bottle, handing it to her. DIANE pours herself a drink.)

DIANE: And me? *(She smiles, lifting the glass to her lips.)* I am what you expected?

(He regards her for a moment.)

MAREK: Yes.

(She smiles, amused.)

DIANE: And is that good?

(Again, he regards her.)

MAREK: Yes.

(Lifting her chin with a provocative smirk, DIANE draws MAREK in for a long, sexy kiss—a signal, if any was needed, that the evening has legs. Then...)

DIANE: I thought so. *(She pulls back, the smile still playing at her face. Then)* So tell me about this place. How did this happen?

MAREK: How..?

DIANE: How did... Did you buy it, do you rent?

MAREK: I built it.

DIANE: *(Surprised)* You built it?

MAREK: Yes. With my father.

DIANE: *(Astonished)* You built this whole place?!

MAREK: *(Laughing)* Yes.

DIANE: This is after communism?

MAREK: This is before communism, during communism.

DIANE: *(Astounded)* You built this?

MAREK: Yes.

DIANE: Jesus. *(She reaches over, touching a window shutter.)*

MAREK: Actually, this is funny story. He did not want it. I had...many friends. I very much wanted...a place to go. So I said to him, "if you will help me, I will leave our apartment. I will give you my room." *(He shrugs.)* And for my room he said yes.

(DIANE remains astounded.)

DIANE: Well, it's really quite beautiful.

(MAREK watches her with amusement, sipping his drink. Then...)

MAREK: I had here my best day of my life. This is in time after University and many people were here. From Prague, from Brno, all of our friends and no one knew why. Of course, we had often friends. That was not unusual. But this time was different. This was *all* our friends. And there was to be an announcement.

Well, at first we did same as always, we sang songs,
drank wine, but then, when night time came, when
it was late, Iva and Jiri drew us together—fifty people
in this room—and told us their secret. That night,
after midnight, they were going to Germany. They
had decided to defect. And they wanted everyone,
all of their friends, all of their closest friends, to
celebrate this last night in the country. The next day,
they said, they would call us. If they made it—they
were going in the trunk of a car—they would call us
the next day from Munich.

(DIANE *is transfixed.*)

DIANE: *(Beat, hushed)* And? Did they?

MAREK: That was our question. All night that was our
question. Would they? And then another question.
"If not, why; why would they not?" And I knew in
my heart the answer. Because someone in this room
had betrayed them. If they were caught...it would mean
someone from our group, people who had known each
other for years, had gone in the middle of the night and
told the police. So that made the next question. "Were
these people my friends? Were they *truly* my friends?"
And I knew I would know the next morning. If the
telephone rang, they were. If it did not...they were not.

DIANE: *(Beat)* Did it?

MAREK: Yes. At noon the next day, it did.

DIANE: *(Relieved)* Jesus.

MAREK: Well, of course, I was happy for them. But you
know what? I was happier even more for us. Because
I knew we had answered a question not many can
answer. "Were our friends truly our friends?" The
answer was yes. For us, it was yes.

*(After a moment, MAREK smiles at DIANE, who looks back at
him shaking her head.)*

DIANE: Amazing.

MAREK: And that's what is missing now. With all the new copiers, the new paint, the big restaurants, with all of capitalism, we no longer have that. To have fifty people in a room, sixty even—and know you can trust every one. Some men don't have that with their wives.

DIANE: *(Archly)* Really?

(MAREK *smiles at her.*)

MAREK: This you know.

DIANE: Yes. This I know.

(Pause)

MAREK: Tell me Diane, does he mind?

DIANE: What?

MAREK: What we are doing.

DIANE: Yes.

MAREK: But...still you do it.

DIANE: Yes.

MAREK: Why?

DIANE: I am younger.

MAREK: And?

DIANE: Those are the rules. Rules an older man lives by.

MAREK: I see.

(Slight pause)

DIANE: You don't. You think I'm unfair.

MAREK: I...am not to judge.

DIANE: What were you going to say?

MAREK: Nothing.

DIANE: You were going to say something. What?

(Slight pause)

MAREK: Perhaps he is angry.

DIANE: And?

MAREK: Perhaps...that is why he behaves as he does.

DIANE: Perhaps.

MAREK: Perhaps...if you were nicer...to him...he would not be so angry.

(Pause)

DIANE: You know, I'm confused.

MAREK: By...?

DIANE: You. A man who has just screwed another man's wife, and now has sympathy for him.

MAREK: I—

DIANE: Pavel, listen to me. Lubo and I have an agreement. We are satisfied. You should be, too.

MAREK: All right.

(Pause)

DIANE: *(Reaching out)* Let's get back to—

MAREK: One more thing. About Lubo. What does he want? Why does he...push so hard?

DIANE: Why do you think?

MAREK: It doesn't make sense. I am only a mayor. I am...there are others more powerful.

DIANE: In some things, yes. In other things, no.

MAREK: In what things, yes?

DIANE: What does a mayor control, Pavel? What does a mayor in the town next to a nuclear plant control?

MAREK: I don't know.

DIANE: Think.

MAREK: *(Shaking his head)* I...I don't know.

DIANE: The ground. He controls the ground. And what is the ground good for?

MAREK: I...

DIANE: Waste. *(She looks at him for a long moment, then continues, whispering...)* It's good for waste. To store waste.

(Pause)

MAREK: The waste is in Dukovany.

DIANE: So they say. But that's over two hundred miles from here. Two hundred miles over badly paved roads meant to carry nothing more frightening than chicken and fruit. And now they'll carry fuel rods? Spent uranium? Truckloads of still fissionable material bumping halfway into Moravia uniting every town along the way in a panic of fear and desperation? How much easier it would be to store it here in the ground. Sealed and fortified. Never to be moved. And all one had to do is convince a single man. The Mayor of Karlovec. *(Beat, quiet)* Do that and you win the contract. Don't do it...and you still have competition.

(MAREK is stunned by her candor.)

MAREK: Why are you telling me this?

DIANE: You asked.

MAREK: But...I cannot say yes.

DIANE: Then you'll say no.

(Beat)

MAREK: And when Lubo finds out?

DIANE: Finds out what?

MAREK: How I learned this.

DIANE: How will he find out?

MAREK: I...

DIANE: There are a million ways you could learn this,
Pavel—not least that he'll have to tell you. In the end,
if he wants your permission...he'll have to tell you.
(Pause) The only way he finds out you learned it from
me...is if you tell *him*. And you won't do that. Will you?

MAREK: No.

DIANE: No. *(Purring)* Because why? Why won't you tell
him?

(She draws him in close.)

MAREK: Because...

DIANE: Because you like what we have here, don't you?
And you know we could have it for some time.

(She pulls him even closer.)

DIANE: Come here.

(And once again they kiss.)

DIANE: *(Hoarse)* Make love to me.

MAREK: I—

DIANE: No talk. Just love.

*(Finding his way under the covers, MAREK is about to
embrace her, when suddenly the door bursts open and
LUBO flies into the room. He is furious.)*

LUBO: All right, so this is what I don't understand.
I call your office and the line is busy. How can that be?
Here you are fucking my wife, and yet someone is in
your office using your phone.

(MAREK rises up, stunned at LUBO's arrival.)

MAREK: It is Alison.

LUBO: Alison?

MAREK: The Congress person.

LUBO: Alison, the Congress person, she is using your phone?

MAREK: *(Halting)* She...asked if she could come to my office, yes. This is how many hours ago?

LUBO: *(Enraged)* This is right now. This is not many hours ago. This is right now.

MAREK: Well, I am surprised, but...yes.

LUBO: Well, you're right. I went by your office, thinking you were there, and instead there was Alison. So I asked where you were and she said maybe here. Isn't that wonderful?

DIANE: *(To MAREK)* You told her you were here?

MAREK: She asked...in case there was problem.

DIANE: *(Incredulous)* You told her you were here!

MAREK: I didn't think it would be now. This was hours ago.

LUBO: Well, it *is* now, Pavel. I am here, and it is now. So what are we doing?

MAREK: *(At a loss)* I...

LUBO: Tell me what we are doing?

MAREK: I...don't know.

LUBO: We are fucking my wife. Aren't we fucking my wife?

MAREK: *(Awkward)* That's...I would like to explain.

LUBO: I would like that. I would like that very much. *(Beat)* Diana, would you do me a great favor and get dressed? *(Tossing her blouse to her)* As beautiful as you

are, I find it distracting to look at your breasts.
(To MAREK*)* Please.

MAREK: I am sorry. I have...I have made a big mistake.

LUBO: Is that right?

MAREK: I...did not think that...

LUBO: You have spent alot of time not thinking,
haven't you?

MAREK: *(Faltering)* I can...perhaps I can... *(Then)*
...what can I do?

LUBO: To me? For me? To make it up to me?

MAREK: Yes.

LUBO: You can't. There is nothing you can do. Even if
you give me the land under your plant—a plan I am
sure Diana has told you about—that would still not
make it up to me. Because you have done something
Pavel that is worse than stealing. You have betrayed a
friend. We were friends, you and I. Weren't we friends?

MAREK: Yes.

LUBO: And yet you didn't think twice about fucking my
wife.

MAREK: I did think twice.

LUBO: You did think twice?

MAREK: *(Reeling)* Yes. I did. But...then...

LUBO: *(Sarcastic)* She proved irresistible. You couldn't
control yourself.

MAREK: Yes.

(Long pause)

LUBO: So what do we do?

MAREK: I don't know.

LUBO: We could call your superiors. How would that be?

MAREK: I—

LUBO: What would they say to you?

MAREK: I don't know.

LUBO: Well, imagine it. Or the ministry in Prague. The trade ministry. How would they talk to you?

MAREK: They would not be pleased.

LUBO: What would they say?

MAREK: They would...I think they would ask—

LUBO: Would they tell you this man you dishonored, this man Lubo Brodsky, he has been to the Castle, he is know throughout government... *(His voice rising throughout)* ...he is here at our invitation???

MAREK: Maybe.

LUBO: Maybe?

MAREK: *(Correcting himself)* Yes.

DIANE: Lubo—

LUBO: Diane! *(To MAREK)* And then what would they say?

MAREK: I don't know.

LUBO: "Do the papers know?" *(In their voice)* They would ask, "do the papers know? The journalists?" And what would you say to that?

MAREK: No. They don't know.

LUBO: "Will he talk, this man Brodsky? He is very upset. Will he talk?"

MAREK: I don't know.

LUBO: *(Bitter, angry)* We'll have to see.

(Suddenly LUBO *whips out a Polaroid, firing off a shot in a bright flash of light.)*

LUBO: *(After a beat)* Just to be safe. *(Then)* Diana.

DIANE: Lubo, don't do this. Don't use that picture.

LUBO: Get dressed.

(In silence, LUBO *then watches as* DIANE *puts on her pants. Quickly she buckles them and soon steps into her shoes. Once she has,* LUBO *looks back at* MAREK *one last time. His eyes burn holes.)*

MAREK: I am sorry.

LUBO: You will have to do better than that. *(Then)* Come Diana.

(And with that, LUBO *leads* DIANE *out the door.)*

(Blackout. End Scene Seven)

Scene Eight

(A hotel room. ALISON *stands at the doorway as* BARRY *pushes past. She follows him with her eyes.)*

ALISON: *(Irked, aggressive)* I don't understand though.

(He turns to face her.)

BARRY: What's not to understand?

ALISON: Why you're here.

BARRY: You think it's unusual?

ALISON: You don't?

BARRY: Not at all.

ALISON: You visit reporters on assignment... *(Peeved)* ...often?

BARRY: All the time.

ALISON: For what purpose?

BARRY: It's a big story.

ALISON: And you don't trust me to write it?

BARRY: You could use some help. *(Beat)*

ALISON: O K. *(Then, an afterthought)* Although I have to tell you...

(BARRY cocks his head.)

ALISON: Never mind.

(Beat)

BARRY: So where are we?

ALISON: I'm not sure. I've met with Brodsky, his wife, the Mayor—

BARRY: *(Breaking in)* His wife?

ALISON: Yes.

BARRY: He has a wife?

ALISON: Yes.

BARRY: And she's here with him?

ALISON: Yes.

(Slight pause. BARRY is puzzled.)

BARRY: Go on.

(During the following exchange BARRY and ALISON bounce off each other, a pair of colleagues working a problem.)

ALISON: I had lunch with them yesterday. Actually, when I first got here the Mayor was there and they were clearly in the middle of conversations, and when I showed up the Mayor immediately wanted to leave. So I left with him. I managed to get him to let me use his office, (I told him I needed the phone), and I went through his files.

BARRY: And?

ALISON: Most was in Czech so it didn't do me much good. But there were a few things in English. One was a notebook from Westinghouse outlining their offer. Another was a file from Greenpeace making clear their objections. A third was a bank check from the United States.

(BARRY *raises his eyebrows.)*

BARRY: A bank check?

ALISON: Drawn on an account in Fort Meade.

BARRY: Bingo.

ALISON: Except it didn't say anything about Temelin.

BARRY: It wouldn't. They'd want to keep it clean. What did it say?

ALISON: Not much. Name of a corporation of some kind, Krauthamer something. And the amount. Fifteen thousand.

BARRY: And the Westinghouse thing, how much is there?

ALISON: Nothing. For him, nothing. A hospital, an apartment block—everything for the village.

BARRY: His thing's the check.

(She shrugs, nodding her head.)

BARRY: And for what exactly? What do they ask for?

ALISON: There's no mention. Dumping rights, we presume, but...there's no mention.

(Pause)

BARRY: What did he say to you? You say you left with him, what did he say?

ALISON: Nothing. About Temelin? Nothing. He talked about the village. About the Americans, all of us here. Not a word about Temelin.

BARRY: All right, well look, we got the bank check. Did you photocopy it?

ALISON: I took it.

BARRY: You what!

ALISON: I didn't know what else to do.

BARRY: Alison—

ALISON: There were no machines, Barry. *(By now she is crossing to her jacket.)*

BARRY: You can't take the check, Alison. What the hell are we gonna do with the check?

ALISON: I—

BARRY: It will look like we planted it.

ALISON: *(Suddenly, confused)* It—

BARRY: *(Impatient)* Here, give it to me. Give it to me!

(She hands him the envelope.)

BARRY: Is it endorsed? *(He quickly opens the envelope.)*

ALISON: What?

BARRY: Is... *(By now he sees the check)* It's not endorsed. *(He laughs, dismissively.)* This is worthless.

(ALISON looks back at him, hurt and in shock.)

BARRY: *(Then, once again working the problem)* O K, well look, we'll deal with this later. Did you find anything else? On Siemens? Tractabel? Other bidders? Anything?

ALISON: Nothing in English.

BARRY: But it could be there?

ALISON: Maybe.

BARRY: *(Impatient, exasperated)* Is that the feeling you got? Is this guy playing one against the other?

ALISON: Not...no. I don't think so.

BARRY: *(Quick)* And what about Lubo?

ALISON: What?

BARRY: Brodsky. What about him? You said you went for lunch.

ALISON: What you'd expect. Very...careful.

BARRY: What did you tell him?

ALISON: About?

BARRY: You.

ALISON: I said I was from Congress. That I was the liaison from Congress.

BARRY: Alison Crawford?

ALISON: *(Confused)* Alis—?

BARRY: Were you Alison Crawford?

ALISON: Yes.

BARRY: *(Annoyed)* Well, that's blown. I'm sure he checked that out. *(Then, pressing on)* And what did you say, as this liaison from Congress?

ALISON: Just...that we were interested. That we wanted Westinghouse to get the bid.

BARRY: And you wanted to see how things were going.

ALISON: Yes.

(Slight pause)

BARRY: And why is he here? Did he tell you?

ALISON: I—

BARRY: I mean, why here and not Prague?

ALISON: He didn't say.

(Beat)

BARRY: The Mayor obviously. Prague's covered.

ALISON: *(Shaking her head, shrugging)* I guess.

(Slight pause)

BARRY: *(Then, eagerly)* You want to know what I found?

ALISON: Sure.

BARRY: Actually, I knew it before, but I just had it confirmed. Brodsky's been in and out of this country a hundred and fifty times since 1981.

ALISON: Meaning?

BARRY: Meaning he left the country in '71 and for ten years he never came back. Then when he came back, he came back a lot.

ALISON: I still don't get it.

BARRY: *(Exasperated)* He leaves in '71. Why?

ALISON: The Russians.

BARRY: *(Nodding)* The politics, right. He's on the side of the angels. But then he comes back ten years later, the same regime is still in power, and they let him back in; they let him back in repeatedly.

ALISON: *(Shaking her head, confused)* I...still—

BARRY: *(Exploding)* Why do they suddenly let this man, whom they earlier expelled, back in???

ALISON: Because—

BARRY: Because he isn't who he said he was. He wasn't a dissident. He was an agent!

ALISON: Of—

BARRY: Of theirs! Of the Communists!

ALISON: *(Shocked)* Brodsky was a Communist?

BARRY: He was an agent. Maybe he was playing both sides, but he was an agent.

ALISON: Whose side is he now?

BARRY: The only side left.

ALISON: Ours.

BARRY: *(Nodding his head)* Westinghouse. And look what he can offer them. He knows people in and out of government on both sides.

(Beat)

ALISON: *(Suspicious)* How do you know all this?

BARRY: I made a few calls.

ALISON: To confirm, you said. You said you knew this all earlier.

BARRY: That's right.

ALISON: *(Hard)* How?

(Beat)

BARRY: You sound like you're onto something.

ALISON: I have a suspicion.

BARRY: Of?

ALISON: You talked to him.

BARRY: *(Beat, thrown)* I told you. He and I worked together.

ALISON: Recently.

BARRY: What makes you say that?

ALISON: How else would you know? *(Beat)* You know so much. How else would you know?

BARRY: *(Beat)* I haven't spoken to him in twenty-two years.

ALISON: *(Aggressive)* When...? *(Slight beat)* What happened?

(BARRY *looks at her coldly.*)

BARRY: My story, on my terms, at my time.

ALISON: Just tell me that. What happened? The last time you saw him.

(BARRY *waits a long moment.*)

BARRY: He got the call.

ALISON: What call?

BARRY: When I was arrested.

ALISON: You were arrested together?

BARRY: *(Intense)* He got the call.

(Beat)

ALISON: I don't understand.

BARRY: *(Short)* Figure it out. *(He stands.)*

ALISON: He set you up.

(Beat)

BARRY: That's what I've always thought. *(Then)* Of course, I didn't have proof then, I don't have proof now. All I know is the list you spoke of, the one I supposedly carried, he carried as well. And shortly after I was arrested, he was arrested, too. The only difference is he's been passing back and forth through the border for more than a decade now—and until the wall came down, I never did.

(ALISON *looks at him suspiciously.*)

ALISON: Who told you this? About Brodsky?

BARRY: Friends. We still have the same friends.

(Beat)

ALISON: And this is why you put me on the story. For revenge.

BARRY: The story's legitimate. If it happens that Brodsky gets hurt, I won't lose sleep over it.

(ALISON stares at him, wondering whether to trust him—and whether to be hurt.)

ALISON: You could have told me.

BARRY: I told you enough.

(By now at the door, BARRY reaches for the knob. A moment passes, as ALISON continues to watch him distrustfully.)

BARRY: Listen, I'm going out for some food. You want me to bring you something?

ALISON: No. Thanks. I'm fine.

(He opens the door.)

ALISON: *(Blurting)* Barry!

(He turns back.)

ALISON: *(Then)* Nothing.

(BARRY laughs.)

BARRY: And for this you don't have your tape.

(With that, BARRY finally exits the room, chuckling as he goes, as ALISON turns furiously to her note pad. And the lights fade slowly to black.)

(End Scene Eight)

Scene Nine

(Once again BARRY *and* LUBO *are facing out, as if on the phone, their conversation as clipped and nervous as before.)*

LUBO: I don't understand.

BARRY: *She* does it.

LUBO: Does what?

BARRY: Applies the pressure. You get her and him and you in the room and she shows it to him.

LUBO: And?

BARRY: And it's the same as me only better. This way it doesn't look like a set-up. This way it looks like she found the check, it's clearly a bribe, and she's busting him for it. He can't wiggle out.

LUBO: And if he does wiggle out? If he says "fuck you?"

BARRY: He won't.

LUBO: If he does.

BARRY: He won't!

LUBO: What if he does!

BARRY: I'm telling you, he won't! Plus you said you got a photograph. What's he gonna do with that?

LUBO: *(Immediate)* I don't like it.

BARRY: Lubo—

LUBO: Barry, I don't want to do this. I want to do what we planned.

BARRY: I can't.

*(*LUBO *is furious.)*

LUBO: What do you mean you can't?

BARRY: I... *(Bravely)* ...it's not possible any more.

(Pause)

LUBO: *(Very cold)* Barry, what are you saying?

BARRY: Lubo, look, you're getting what you want. We're just doing it a different way.

(LUBO considers this. a moment passes.)

LUBO: So how does this work? She shows him the check—

BARRY: And she points out where it's from. *She* makes the connection to C D I.

LUBO: And?

BARRY: He caves. The moment he realizes, he caves.

LUBO: And if he doesn't?

BARRY: We put on more pressure. We tell him I'm going to print it.

LUBO: And?

BARRY: And again, I think he caves. If he doesn't, we get his people on the line. Hase... *(About to say "Hasek", he stops.)* ...actually, now that I think of it, we do that first. They want to get rid of him, you said. Isn't that what you said? That they're looking for a reason to get rid of him?

LUBO: *(Cautious)* Yes.

BARRY: So this is it. We get Hasek, Holub on the line, we tell them what he's done, they get rid of him. We're in.

(Beat)

LUBO: And the reason for the girl?

BARRY: I said, she's more credible.

LUBO: Barry... *(His tone hardening)* ...the reason for the girl?

(This last he says impatiently, wanting to cut through the B S . And BARRY *swallows, nervously, taking a moment before answering.)*

BARRY: *(Then, finally)* She knows.

LUBO: Knows what?

BARRY: Everything. *(Beat)* Or nearly everything. She knows what we did.

LUBO: And?

(Pause)

BARRY: I need you to help me.

LUBO: In what way?

BARRY: *(Plaintive)* Tell her I'm innocent.

LUBO: *(Taunting)* But you're not.

BARRY: But tell her I am.

LUBO: But you're not.

BARRY: *(Angry)* But I am, goddammit! I am! *(His fury overflowing)* I mean, my God, Lubo, all these years I've done nothing wrong except for you. Except for when you called. Other than that I've done nothing. NOTHING! *(Near tears now, beside himself)* And yet I've had to pay for it. I've had to pay for it endlessly. And now, finally, I'm asking you to help me, goddammit! Help me!

*(*LUBO *waits for a moment.)*

LUBO: *(Then, coolly)* And in return?

*(*BARRY *tries to gather himself.)*

BARRY: *(Thrown)* What?

LUBO: In return? What do I get?

(BARRY *needs still another moment to gather himself.*)

BARRY: You get what you want. We all get what we want. You get Temelin, she gets her story...I get my life back.

(*At this, a long moment passes.*)

LUBO: O K. (*Then, immediately*) But Barry...don't mistake what I'm doing here. I'm not doing you a favor. I'm making you a deal.

(*Beat*)

BARRY: (*Quiet*) I know.

(*Beat*)

LUBO: Remember it.

(*Blackout. End Scene Nine*)

Scene Ten

(*The sitting room of the hunting lodge. From the hallway offstage comes the sound of* MAREK'*s voice yelling in outrage.*)

MAREK: (*Off*) How can you do this? Please tell me, how you can do this???

(LUBO *enters with* MAREK *right behind him, enraged.* LUBO, *on the other hand, is quite calm.*)

LUBO: (*Strong*) I am a man in my home. I—

MAREK: You are not in your home! This is not your home! You are a tourist!

(LUBO *stops at the landing, his tone utterly self-righteous.*)

LUBO: So long as I am living here, this is my home.

MAREK: You are hurting my life.

LUBO: You are hurting *my* life. *(He continues into the room.)*

MAREK: Lubo, it is not just me you are hurting. You are hurting my people.

LUBO: No, Pavel, you forget. I am helping your people. I am *trying* to *help* your people.

(Pause. MAREK stares at him.)

MAREK: How did you learn of this?

LUBO: Learn of what?

MAREK: This check.

LUBO: It is from my company.

MAREK: *(Outraged)* It is not from your company!

LUBO: *(Calling)* Miss Crawford?

(LUBO turns back to the stairway just as ALISON appears from behind it. She has been listening to them.)

MAREK: *(Horrified)* What are you doing here?

ALISON: I found the check. I came to ask about it.

MAREK: You found the check?

ALISON: In your office, yes.

MAREK: You found the check in my office!

ALISON: Drawn on an account from Fort Meade. Yes.

(With this, she pulls out the check, holding it up to him.)

ALISON: It says, clearly—"Fort Meade".

(MAREK is panicking.)

MAREK: The check is for a cemetery. *(His voice is starting to rise.)* Would you like me to tell you what that check is for?

LUBO: I have told her.

MAREK: It is for a cemetery! A Jewish cemetery! I am trying to restore a Jewish cemetery that for fifty years has been abandoned! *(He stops, trying to calm himself)* A man visited me last month. A man from America. He gave me that check to help me with the cemetery!

ALISON: It is made out to you.

MAREK: Well, of course, it is made out to me. Why not?!?

ALISON: How do I know it's to be used for a cemetery?

MAREK: You know because I tell you. You... *(Suddenly, exploding)* ...besides, why you must know! Who are you that you must know!

LUBO: I am afraid Miss Crawford has not been honest with us. She is not from the Congress. She is from *The Prague Star.*

(At this, MAREK simply stares at her, unable to speak.)

LUBO: The American newspaper? *(Beat)* She is from there.

(And then suddenly MAREK understands.)

MAREK: It is you who have made the calls. You made the calls?

ALISON: Yes.

MAREK: Why?

(She shrugs.)

ALISON: The story is important.

MAREK: What story!!

ALISON: The story of you and Mister Brodsky.

MAREK: There *is* no story of me and Mister Brodsky!

LUBO: Pavel—

MAREK: Lubo, please, tell her. Tell her there is no story.

LUBO: I did. She doesn't believe me.

ALISON: How else do you explain the check?

MAREK: I told you. The check is from another man. A man from America.

LUBO: Martin Krauthamer.

MAREK: Yes!

(With that, MAREK suddenly whirls around on LUBO.)

MAREK: *(Amazed)* How do you know that?

LUBO: Perhaps we should sit. *(He gestures to the couch.)*

MAREK: *(Incensed, louder)* How do you know that!

ALISON: He works for Mister Brodsky.

MAREK: Who does?

LUBO: Mister Krauthamer.

ALISON: He runs a company called Krauthamer Micronics. A wholly owned subsidiary of C D I.

MAREK: *(Repeating, lost)* A wholly...owned...?

(Again LUBO gestures...)

LUBO: Perhaps we should sit.

(...and this time, reluctantly, MAREK goes to the couch.)

LUBO: It is true what she says. I do own this company. And it is true also that Mister Krauthamer works for me. But what comes of that, what we will *make* of that...that is unclear. Perhaps you can help me.

MAREK: *(Light-headed, reeling)* I don't understand.

LUBO: Pavel, you are a good man. You want what is best for your town, for your people. I know that. And I think I can explain it to Miss Crawford. Unfortunately...it is not so simple this problem. We have also to convince others. These people she has called, and I have called—I, too, have made calls—these people must also be convinced. And that will not be easy. We will need your help.

(Pause. LUBO *peers deeply at* MAREK, *his look both serious and concerned.)*

LUBO: Will you help?

MAREK: *(Confused)* I...I...

LUBO: Pavel, look, there is something you should know. Miss Crawford is interested in Karlovec, yes. But she is also interested in me. If I tell her my story, she may not want to write yours. She may even call up the minister, the head of your party, and tell them she got it wrong. That you and I have *not* made arrangements. That I did *not* give you a...what did she call it, "bribe".

MAREK: *(Aghast)* You didn't!

LUBO: And I think I can convince her of that.

MAREK: If... *(Feeling queasy)* ...what?

LUBO: We can reach an understanding.

(Slight pause)

MAREK: About?

LUBO: This "issue" we've been discussing. Our problem.

(Pause)

MAREK: *(To* ALISON*)* Will you do what he says? Will you call back Hasek?

ALISON: *(Nodding)* I'll call back Hasek and Holub. I will tell them I got it wrong.

(Pause)

MAREK: All right.

LUBO: You'll do it.

MAREK: Yes.

LUBO: Good.

MAREK: On one condition. *(Beat)* I must first return to my office.

LUBO: For what?

MAREK: To see my files.

LUBO: *(Annoyed)* What files?

MAREK: On Krauthamer. I wrote notes. I want to see them.

LUBO: Pavel—

MAREK: I insist on seeing them! *(Then, softer)* I will be twenty minutes.

LUBO: *(Then)* Twenty minutes?

MAREK: Yes.

(Beat)

LUBO: All right.

(And instantly MAREK is out of his chair.)

LUBO: But Pavel!

(MAREK stops, commanded by LUBO's voice.)

LUBO: ...that's all.

(Then instantly MAREK is gone. Once he has left, LUBO is on his feet, speaking in a tone of extreme, frightening urgency.)

LUBO: Where is my wife?

ALISON: What?

LUBO: My wife, where did she go! *(He is practically screaming.)*

ALISON: I don't know.

LUBO: I must find her.

ALISON: *(Blurting)* I'll print this.

(Starting for the stairs, LUBO *suddenly turns back.)*

LUBO: *(Alarmed)* What?

ALISON: If you duck me, I'll print this.

LUBO: Darling, I am not "ducking" you. I am trying to find my wife.

ALISON: I want to talk about Barry.

LUBO: Later.

ALISON: Now! *(She stands, firm.)* That was our deal. Now.

LUBO: Darling—

ALISON: Mister Brodsky, I'm not joking. You tell me about Barry or I write about you. I write about this deal.

LUBO: May I speak to Alison Crawford, please? *(This last he says as if speaking into a telephone, miming a handset. He is speaking in a different voice. his tone is insidious.)* It is Franticek Dudek.

*(*ALISON *starts—startled and speechless.)*

ALISON: *(Stunned)* What?

LUBO: *(Slowly)* Franticek Dudek. I have an interesting story to tell her.

(She stares, still confused.)

ALISON: You... *(Then, starting to understand)* ...it was you?

LUBO: Yes.

ALISON: You told me about Barry?

LUBO: Yes.

ALISON: Why?

LUBO: That, I must say, is a bit complicated. Suffice it to say, I had my reasons. As I have my reasons now. *(Then)* But—

ALISON: Look, I... *(Suddenly upset)* ...can't do this.

LUBO: *(Annoyed)* Why not?

ALISON: Because I don't understand what's going on!

LUBO: *(Angry, abrupt)* Then let me explain it to you. You are about to get a story that will make your career. That will resonate throughout Europe. That... But only if you follow my lead. Otherwise, I won't give it to you. *(Then, quieter)* It's as simple as that.

(ALISON stares at him, still putting together the pieces.)

ALISON: *You* called me?

LUBO: Yes.

ALISON: And set Barry up.

LUBO: I told Barry's story.

ALISON: That he carried the list.

LUBO: Yes.

(Beat)

ALISON: And that's true?

LUBO: It is, yes.

ALISON: How do you know that?

LUBO: Because I gave it to him.

ALISON: You... *(Thrown)* ...what?

LUBO: We were putting together a journal he and I. This was a list of our subscribers. I gave it to him in his apartment.

ALISON: And?

LUBO: Had him arrested with it.

ALISON: You what?!?

LUBO: I made sure the police knew where he was going and when he was getting there. And when he got there...they arrested him.

ALISON: Why?

LUBO: Because they asked me to.

ALISON: Who did?

LUBO: The police. I had been arrested weeks earlier and I was going to prison. If I had him arrested...I would go free. *(Then)* Alison, look, it's a complicated story, but one, I assure you, that will garner you great fame, if—and this is important—you know the rest of the story. So far you know only what happened *before* he was arrested. What's interesting...is what happened after.

ALISON: What?

LUBO: That I will only tell you if we have a deal. *(Beat)* Do we?

ALISON: Do—?

LUBO: I give you Barry. You forget Mister Marek.

(Beat)

ALISON: Mister—

LUBO: I am serious, Alison. I don't want to be threatened by you. I give you what you want, what you came here for...and you forget what has happened between me and the Mayor. Which, after all, is little more than mere politics. As you have seen, he did not take this bribe. He is an honest man.

ALISON: And you are not.

LUBO: No, I...but then, I am gone. Once this is over, I am gone. So you have a choice. You can either write a story about a man who is gone—which will have little impact because Temelin will be built one way or the other... *(He takes a moment)* ...or you can write a story that is truthful, that is honest, that goes to the very heart of what it's meant to live in this country for the last forty years. *(Beat)* Your choice...as I say.

(Beat)

ALISON: I won't do again what I did just now. I won't be involved.

(LUBO simply stares at her.)

ALISON: What happened after?

LUBO: Do we have a deal?

(Beat)

ALISON: Yes.

(LUBO nods.)

LUBO: Ask him about U Kralu.

ALISON: What?

LUBO: U Kralu. Ask him about that. See what he says.

ALISON: What will he say?

LUBO: See. *(With that, he stands...)* And in the meantime...if you'll excuse me... *(...And starts for the stairs.)*

ALISON: She was waiting for him.

LUBO: *(Turning, confused)* What?

ALISON: Your wife. Outside. She was waiting.

LUBO: Fuck! *(And with that, he bolts up the stairs and out the door, his movements as fast and impetuous as they were earlier slow and controlled.)*

(And for a long moment, ALISON simply stares after him.)

(Blackout. End Scene Ten)

Scene Eleven

(MAREK's office. MAREK and DIANE enter in a rush.

DIANE: *(Panicked)* You can't fight him this way.

MAREK: What do you mean?

DIANE: In the open. This isn't a democracy. This—

MAREK: Stand over there. *(He points to a window as he crosses to a closet.)*

DIANE: *(Off-guard)* What?

MAREK: By the window.

DIANE: What are you doing?

MAREK: A trick.

DIANE: What kind of trick?

MAREK: An old one.

DIANE: Pavel—

MAREK: *(Impatient)* Diane, just stand by the window, will you? Please!

(MAREK turns back to the closet as DIANE finally goes to the window.)

DIANE: You have to call someone.

MAREK: Who?

DIANE: Someone with power.

MAREK: Who?

DIANE: The man at the Ministry. Whatsisname? Holub.

MAREK: He isn't my friend.

DIANE: Well, your party boss. Ha—*(About to say "Hasek")*

MAREK: He isn't my friend either.

DIANE: Pavel—

(*Suddenly* MAREK *emerges, practically ranting in frustration.*)

MAREK: Diane, listen to me. All that has stood between us and this plant has been me. For months now, since I came here, it's been me. Me and these mayors! Now, please, look out the window! (*This last he says emphatically, pointing—before heading back to the closet.*)

DIANE: I just—

MAREK: Besides, he wants to make Temelin more than your husband.

DIANE: Who does?

MAREK: Hasek. (*And once again, he is busy, doing something just out of sight.*)

DIANE: (*Then, after a beat*) He isn't my husband.

MAREK: (*Re-emerging, alarmed*) What?

DIANE: (*She reconsiders.*) Never mind.

MAREK: What are you talking about?

DIANE: Pavel, listen to me, this whole thing is a set-up. The check is a set-up. You have to tell that to Hasek.

MAREK: For what reason?

DIANE: So that he'll stop this! Tell that to Hasek and I'll tell him the rest.

MAREK: The rest of what?

DIANE: Everything.

(MAREK'*s eyes narrow.*)

MAREK: What do you mean "everything"?

DIANE: *(Slight beat, nervous)* The man you call
Krauthamer doesn't exist. His real name's Axelrod.
Barry Axelrod. He runs *The Prague Star.*

MAREK: *The Prague..?*

DIANE: *(Impatient) Star. (Slight beat)* The American
newspaper? Surely you know it.

MAREK: I know it.

DIANE: Well, he runs it. And he and Lubo have been
working together for months now. They set up this
check as a sting, "the bribing of a mayor." They've been
planning this thing from the start.

MAREK: *(Suspicious)* Why are you telling me this?

DIANE: What?

MAREK: Why are you telling me this?

DIANE: Because I want to help you.

MAREK: WHY!!!

(She stares at him.)

DIANE: *(Then)* Because I love you. I think.

MAREK: *(Incredulous)* You what???

DIANE: *(Nervous)* I...think I love you.

MAREK: You must be joking.

DIANE: I'm not joking.

MAREK: You must be.

DIANE: I'm not! *(Beat)* Pavel, look, I don't expect you to
believe me, and I don't even...maybe it isn't true, maybe
I don't love you. But it sure as hell feels that way. And I
want you to know that.

(At this, MAREK stares at her, a long moment passing.)

MAREK: *(Then, finally)* All right.

DIANE: *(Irked)* All right?

MAREK: *(Irked as well)* All right, yes. Diane, what do you want me to say?

DIANE: How 'bout "I love you, too." Something... *(Now, really annoyed)* ...I don't know! Something nice!

MAREK: No. "All right" is the best I can do. But now, Diane, this man. Who is he?

DIANE: Which man?

MAREK: This man you say isn't your husband. Lubo. Who is he?

DIANE: Pavel—

MAREK: Diane, you must tell me that. If you want to be helpful, you must tell me that.

(Beat)

DIANE: He's my boss. *(Beat)* He's the man I work for.

MAREK: He's... *(He takes a step back, momentarily thrown. Then, with a whistle...)* Jesus Maria.

DIANE: Don't be angry.

MAREK: I'm not.

DIANE: You are.

MAREK: I'm not, I'm... *(Slight beat)* I'm not. *(Then, suddenly, looking around)* I'm just trying to think what to do.

DIANE: We have to get out of here.

MAREK: What?

DIANE: We have to get out of here!

MAREK: No, we don't. We... *(Then suddenly, forcefully)* Here, stand by the window.

DIANE: What?

MAREK: Stand by the window.

DIANE: Pavel—

MAREK: Diane, please, just do what I say! Stand by the window! (*And with that, he quickly ducks into the closet.*) I will be one minute. (*He then quickly comes out again.*)

MAREK: Actually, I have to call someone.

(*But before he can get to his desk,* DIANE *blurts out...*)

DIANE: He's coming!

MAREK: What?

DIANE: (*Pointing outside, panicking*) That's him, right there. He's coming!

MAREK: Stand over here.

DIANE: Pavel—

MAREK: No, you are right. Stand there.

DIANE: I—

MAREK: (*Cutting her off*) Diane, please...just... Don't talk! (*Having crossed to his desk, he quickly dials a number.*)

MAREK: (*Into phone*) Tady Marek. Ano. Dekuji. Dve minuty, prosim. Ano. (*"Marek here. Yes. Thanks. Two minutes, please. Yes."*)

(*This last he says quickly, slamming down the phone. He then turns suddenly to* DIANE.)

MAREK: Doing what?

DIANE: What?

MAREK: You say you worked for him. Doing what? What—

(*But before he can continue,* LUBO *appears in the doorway.*)

LUBO: Whatever I asked.

(*He then quickly looks at* DIANE, *his eyes bright with anger.*)

LUBO: And right now I ask that you leave us, Diana.

MAREK: Diane, stay! Don't go.

(Debating whether or not to leave, DIANE decides to lean back against the desk. When she does this, LUBO smiles, barely concealing his rage.)

LUBO: Well now. Isn't that interesting? She obeys you.

(Continuing to stare at her, he then suddenly turns on MAREK, his manner when he does so oddly playful.)

LUBO: So all right, we have a problem. What do we do?

MAREK: I have called back Hasek and Holub. I have told them what you have done.

LUBO: And?

MAREK: *(Thrown)* I—

LUBO: What did they say?

(Beat)

MAREK: *(Nervous)* They will call back.

LUBO: And? What *will* they say?

MAREK: *(Unsure)* I—

LUBO: Pavel, these are your people. What will they say when they hear you've been bribed?

MAREK: *(Angry)* I have not been bribed!

LUBO: You most certainly have.

MAREK: That check is no good!

LUBO: It was found in your office.

MAREK: I didn't take it as a bribe!

LUBO: But the fact is you took it, Pavel! *(Beat, insistent)* Didn't you? Didn't you take it?!

MAREK: *(Crestfallen, trapped)* Yes.

LUBO: And what's to say you don't have other checks, other money, we so far haven't found? This man in town here, for instance, Vacha I think his name is, he has given you a great deal of money.

MAREK: That's a lie.

LUBO: That's what he tells me.

MAREK: That's a lie!

LUBO: Why would he tell me that?

(LUBO *holds out his hands, circling* MAREK'*s desk.*)

MAREK: (*Backing away*) Because he's a Communist. He wants—

LUBO: He is a builder, he says. He wants to have contracts.

MAREK: He has not given me money!

LUBO: But you see how the water becomes muddy. (*He smiles.*) Don't you?

(*By now he has pushed* MAREK *back into his chair.*)

LUBO: There are others, Pavel. Besides Vacha, besides me. You have made enemies.

(*And* MAREK *stares back at him, speaking when he does in a tone that is both angry and frightened.*)

MAREK: You are right. I have made enemies. And you are right also when you say Holub and Hasek will not believe me. They want, I know, this Temelin. And I'm sure they will get it. After all, I am only one mayor, and the others...I know there are others...who are not anymore on my side. But *I*... (*Beat, gathering himself*) ...you see, this is the point, *I* am here. I live here. (*By now almost crying*) This is *my* town. (*Stopping, steeling himself*) And if I did not before...oppose you...I would now. I will not let you to do this to my country.

LUBO: Unfortunately... *(He smiles.)* ...you don't have a choice.

BARRY: Oh no? Fuck you, Lubo! *(With that, he enters from the anteroom. He is enraged.)*

LUBO: *(Shocked)* Barry—

BARRY: *(Calling out)* Alison!

LUBO: What are you doing here?

BARRY: What I should have done years ago.

(MAREK looks at BARRY as if seeing a ghost.)

MAREK: *(To himself, whispered)* Krauthamer.

BARRY: *(Overlapping, sharply)* Ask him your question.

(This last he says to ALISON, who has now joined him in the doorway.)

ALISON: What does he mean, "Krauthamer"?

BARRY: *(Ignoring her)* Ask him what you asked me.

ALISON: Barry, what does he mean by Krauthamer?

BARRY: I'll tell you in a second! First ask him your question!

LUBO: *(Enraged)* Barry, this isn't the time.

BARRY: *(Continuing, to ALISON)* It all stems from that.

LUBO: *(Hot)* Barry, not now!

ALISON: *(To LUBO, impulsive)* What's U Kralu?

(With that, BARRY stares daggers at LUBO, who stares back at him dumbfounded.)

BARRY: *(Coldly)* What is U Kralu, Lubo?

(Beat)

LUBO: *(Tense)* Why are you doing this?

BARRY: *(Hot)* Why do you think?

LUBO: *(Threatening)* So that you can go back to Austria?

BARRY: So I can pull your nails out of my back.

LUBO: Barry—

BARRY: What is U Kralu, Lubo?

(LUBO continues to stare at him.)

LUBO: *(Seething)* The place where we met.

BARRY: And?

LUBO: Had an adventure.

BARRY: And?

LUBO: *(Exploding, desperate)* Barry, why are you doing this? What is the point?

BARRY: Why did you send her to me?

LUBO: I had to get rid of her! I had to get back to Marek!

BARRY: But why tell her about U Kralu?

LUBO: So—

BARRY: *(In a rage)* So you could keep me on a string! Right!?! So you could tell me without saying it in so many words that I was still yours; that I'd better do things the way you want; that I'd better not, for one minute, think of betraying you. *(His eyes burning with fury)* Right?

LUBO: Barry, she didn't believe me. When I told her your story—

BARRY: *(Cutting him off, to* ALISON*)* Shall I tell you what U Kralu is?

LUBO: *(Interceding)* Barry, don't—

BARRY: The place where I lost my soul.

LUBO: That's—

BARRY: The place where I turned in a woman I had known since my twenties, a woman I had been in love with—

LUBO: Barry, I—

BARRY: *(Shouting over him)* ...because Lubo said I had to.

LUBO: *(Beat, nervous)* That's—

BARRY: *(TO ALISON)* You asked what I did in Salzburg all those years; that's what I did. On three separate—

LUBO: *(Exploding)* Barry, stop it, will you? Just stop it! *(Then)* Now, listen to me—

BARRY: Her name was Sarka Rebanova.

(By now the two men are staring at each other, BARRY especially breathing quite heavily.)

LUBO: *(Warning)* Barry—

BARRY: *(Cutting him off)* And after I got her arrested, after I sat down with her and by doing so got her arrested... *(His eyes welling up with tears, emotional)* ...Lubo had her taken away. *(Beat, hard)* And the next thing I heard she had hanged herself.

LUBO: *(Blurting)* She *did* hang herself.

BARRY: Because of you, Lubo! Because of what *you* did to her! You're even more guilty in this than I am. *(Then, after a pause, turning to ALISON... Bitter)* That's what U Kralu is.

(There is another pause.)

LUBO: Look—

BARRY: I'm writing about this, Lubo.

LUBO: About what?

BARRY: Us. Our story. The story of waiting twenty years for your knock and knowing it would always come. Of knowing that no matter how many years intervened, you would always come back. There would always be another day, another assignment I couldn't say no to.

LUBO: I—

BARRY: *(To the others)* Until three months ago, when Lubo again came back, this time working for Westinghouse, and again carried the same message— "you better".

LUBO: That's—

BARRY: *(Exploding, furious)* That's what, Lubo? What is that?

LUBO: I—

BARRY: You didn't say you would call the authorities? That you would tell them what I'd done? You didn't *say* that???

LUBO: I didn't mean that.

BARRY: What did you mean?

LUBO: *(Grasping)* We had a shared history...we—

BARRY: There is no other explanation, Lubo. You were blackmailing me then, you're blackmailing me now. The only difference is this time I'm hitting you back.

LUBO: To what effect? *(Lashing out, bitter)* All right, fine, so you tell them what I've done. So what? Do you think it will stop Temelin?

BARRY: *(Beat)* That—

LUBO: Do you think for one minute the people who want this to happen, Hasek, Holub, will give a shit about me? They will forget in a day. They will kick me out and forget in a day. And then they will kick *you* out, Barry. You see, that's the thing. They will have an excuse then to kick you out, and they will use it!

MAREK: Perhaps not.

LUBO: *(Impatient)* Pavel, please.

MAREK: You may be surprised.

LUBO: Pavel—

MAREK: We *all* may be surprised. *(By now he is on his feet.)*

LUBO: *(Worried)* What are you doing?

MAREK: You said to me one time I sounded like a Communist.

LUBO: Pavel—

MAREK: That I *thought* like one, you said.

LUBO: I—

MAREK: And I remember at the time thinking you were wrong. That...and I was angry that you said it. *(He is by now at his desk.)*

MAREK: But now I think perhaps you were right. At least a little bit right. *(He smiles, rueful.)* And I am sorry for it. *(With that, he raises the phone.)*

LUBO: What are you doing?

(MAREK holds up a finger.)

MAREK: *(Into phone)* Postau Chrta Ven. Zachni Pashu. *("Put Chrt at the door. Start the tape.")*

LUBO: Pavel—

MAREK: Quiet! Please. *(He points.)* And listen.

(All four look at each other, not knowing what he means, when suddenly the sound of a recording is heard.)

BARRY'S VOICE: *(Cutting him off)* Shall I tell you what U Kralu is?

LUBO'S VOICE: Barry, don't—

BARRY'S VOICE: The place where I lost my soul.

(LUBO *looks around, panicking.*)

LUBO: Turn it off.

LUBO'S VOICE: That's—

BARRY'S VOICE: The place where I turned in a woman I had known since my twenties, a woman I had been in love with—

LUBO'S VOICE: Barry, I—

BARRY'S VOICE: *(Continuing, shouting)* ...because Lubo said I *had* to.

LUBO: I said, turn it off!

LUBO'S VOICE: That's—

BARRY'S VOICE: You asked me what I did in Salzburg all those years; that's what I did. On three separate—

LUBO: Goddammit, turn it off!

LUBO'S VOICE: *(Overlapping)* Barry, stop it, will you? Just stop it!

(MAREK *is again on the phone.*)

MAREK: *Dekuji.? ("Thanks.")*

LUBO'S VOICE: Now listen to me—

BARRY'S VOICE: Her name was Sarka Rebanova.

(*And as suddenly as it started, the tape once again shuts off.*)

LUBO: *(Dry-mouthed, panicked)* It proves nothing.

MAREK: It proves a great deal.

LUBO: I have said nothing I would not say again.

MAREK: What you have said is not important. What is said about you...is.

(*Beat*)

LUBO: Sarka Rebanova.

(MAREK *nods.*)

MAREK: *(Cold, deliberate)* If she died...and you were in fact responsible... *(With a triumphant glint)* ...you must answer for it.

(LUBO *stares at him for a long moment, his anger building as he does.*)

LUBO: *(Then)* So I lose, is that it? *(Aggressive)* I lose?

(MAREK *watches him, quietly.*)

MAREK: I—

LUBO: Pavel, please, don't be shy. Shout it out when you win. That's the way it is in the new world. You shout it out! *(Bitter, glaring, he continues.)* Except you don't, do you? Because you are not in the new world. You are in the past. You see, that's the thing. You are a Communist. I hoped you were not, but you are. *(He looks around.)* And it comes not in this. This is... *(He waves dismissively at the hidden microphones above him.)* It comes in this. *(He points to his head.)* It's what's in your head. And in your head, you have what they all have. Fear. Fear of tomorrow. *(His anger building to the end)* You see, that's the irony. That this philosophy that is supposedly so modern, so forward-looking is actually nothing of the sort. It's afraid. It's afraid like an old woman is afraid. Sneaking out of the house hoping tomorrow will not be different. But it *will* be, Pavel. It will be different. And the future will belong to those who can embrace that. Who are not afraid of change. Who can teach themselves, and their children, and their nation... *(By now spitting mad)* ...that we are powerful, that we are resilient, that we have intelligence. That we are not some pathetic disaster of a country so backward and fearful we must hide from progress. *(He studies* MAREK *for a long moment. He smiles.)*

LUBO: But perhaps I am wrong. Maybe we are just as backward and fearful as you think. *(Then, after)* In any case... *(He starts out.)*

MAREK: Where are you going?

LUBO: *(Turning, light)* Are you keeping me?

MAREK: I am, yes.

LUBO: On what authority?

MAREK: Perhaps you have forgotten. I am the Mayor here. And I have asked a police officer to wait for you.

(With that, he gestures to the office outside, and when LUBO looks over he realizes he is trapped. He then looks back at MAREK, resigned, and laughs.)

LUBO: Well, well.

(And with that, he exits. Once he has, MAREK turns to BARRY.)

MAREK: As for you, Mister..?

BARRY: Axelrod.

MAREK: Axelrod. I will contact your embassy and tell them what you have done. I will also, however, suggest they take no action.

BARRY: *(Beat)* And your own government?

MAREK: I will contact them as well.

BARRY: And they'll ask me to leave.

MAREK: They'll...yes, I think you are right.

BARRY: *(Beat)* I see.

(The two men exchange a long look before MAREK suddenly turns on the women breaking into a smile.)

MAREK: As for you ladies...and you too if you like... *(This last he says to BARRY)* ...perhaps you will join me for lunch.

ALISON: *(Interrupting)* Just... *(Outraged)* ...I'm sorry, but am I the only one here who...? *(She turns to* BARRY.*)* You set her up. Right?

BARRY: *(Off balance)* What?

ALISON: This woman you loved. The love of your life. You set her up. *(This last she says disparagingly.)*

BARRY: *(Uncomfortable)* Yes.

ALISON: *(Incredulous)* And all for a job?

BARRY: I—

ALISON: I mean, maybe I'm missing something, but...the way I'm hearing it you turned somebody in, someone you *loved*, so that you could...what, start a newspaper?

*(*BARRY *is silent. The entire room is.)*

ALISON: I mean, tell me, am I missing something here?

*(*BARRY *shakes his head.)*

ALISON: *(Then, after a moment)* And you knew what would happen, didn't you? I mean, this fiction that you didn't *know* what would happen... *(Beat, quiet, outraged)* ...you finger someone for the police...you *know* what will happen.

*(*BARRY *looks back at her in silence. She turns to* MAREK.*)*

ALISON: No, I'm sorry, I'm not sitting at lunch with a man like this. *(Beat)* But thanks for the invite. *(And with that, she starts out—only to suddenly stop.)*

ALISON: Actually...one more thing. For you. *(She turns to* MAREK*)* This system... *(Gesturing above her)* ...you always use this?

MAREK: *(Embarrassed)* No.

ALISON: What...? *(She shakes her head, clearly troubled— as if to say "explain yourself.")*

MAREK: *(After a moment)* When I became Mayor, I found this machine and I asked what it was. What... And nobody knew. Nobody could answer. And then one day I found the answer. It began...as I think they all did...as a...how do you call it...listening device. But it was for the others to listen to the mayor. The secret police. *(Embarrassed)* But then one mayor, I don't know who, maybe it was the one before me...he decided he too would like to listen. So he had the speakers put in so he could play back. *(Pause. Truly saddened)* I never thought I would use such a thing.

ALISON: But now you have.

MAREK: Yes. *(Sadder still)* Now I have.

(Beat. ALISON nods.)

ALISON: Careful, Mister Marek. Careful.

(And with that, on her high horse, she leaves—not looking back as she goes. And a moment passes in silence.)

DIANE: *(Then, finally, fumbling)* I think...what she says—

MAREK: She's right. *(At this, he turns to her.)*

MAREK: She is right.

(And it's clear he's been deeply hurt by ALISON's charge. Another moment then passes.)

BARRY: Maybe so. *(Then, after a pause)* But it's easy for her to say so. She's an American.

DIANE: Meaning what? *(She sounds almost offended.)*

BARRY: Meaning it's never so easy. As Americans think it is. *(Turning back to MAREK)* It's always a little more complicated.

MAREK: *(Rueful smile)* So we say. *(There is another awkward silence.)* You know...I think perhaps we should postpone this lunch. If you understand what I...

(Beat. BARRY *nods.)*

BARRY: I do. *(Then, after a moment, gesturing)* May I...?

MAREK: By all means. You are free.

(And with this, BARRY *quickly exits, nodding briefly to* DIANE *on his way out. Then, once he's gone, there is another silence—and* MAREK *turns to* DIANE, *wondering why she too has not left.)*

MAREK: Yes?

DIANE: What about me?

MAREK: You too are free.

DIANE: No, I'm...I mean, what about me?

(Beat)

MAREK: I don't understand.

DIANE: I'm...

(She stops, unable to continue. MAREK *doesn't help her.)*

DIANE: I thought...

(But still he doesn't answer.)

DIANE: Pavel, I have feelings for you! *(A slight beat)* Don't you have feelings for me?

*(*MAREK *laughs, unable to believe her nerve.)*

MAREK: You know, Diane...you are truly remarkable.

(Beat)

DIANE: What do you mean?

(Again he laughs, this time more fully.)

DIANE: *(Offended)* Why are you laughing???

MAREK: You know, my dear, you have said many things to me...these past few days—and I have often believed you. And that was a mistake. I should *never*...believe you. What I should do instead... *(Coming to her, stopping right at her side)* ...is to simply enjoy you... *(His face now inches from hers)* ...and hope that you are so distracted by our pleasure...that you will not discover a new trick. *(Smiling, his eyes dancing with pleasure as he studies her face)* Is that a good plan?

(DIANE nods, unable to speak.)

DIANE: *(Then, breathless)* Yes.

MAREK: Good.

(With that, he suddenly kisses her. It's a playful, stolen, somewhat abrupt kiss that is no sooner started than finished. And again MAREK smiles, almost laughing.)

MAREK: Come. Let's have lunch.

DIANE: But—

MAREK: No more for now. For now, we must eat. *(He then crosses to the doorway, speaking as he goes.)*

MAREK: The restaurant next door is wonderful. The carp is delicious.

(He then turns back to her, holding out his hand. And after a moment, she comes to him, her voice when she reaches him enormously earnest.)

DIANE: I do care for you, you know.

(And MAREK once again smiles, almost laughing.)

MAREK: I know.

(And with that, he sweeps her through the door—and the lights, very slowly, fade to black.)

(End Scene Eleven)

END OF PLAY

www.ingramcontent.com/pod-product-compliance
Lightning Source LLC
Chambersburg PA
CBHW052117090426
42741CB00009B/1851